1st and 2nd

Corinthians

Letters of Correction

Part of A Devotional Commentary Series

By Lou Nicholes

xulon
PRESS

I & II Corinthians
Letters of Correction
by Lou Nicholes

Printed in the United States of America

ISBN 1-594674-48-5

Unless otherwise indicated Scripture quotations are from the *King James Version* of the Bible.

Proof Reading by Mary Sack

www.xulonpress.com

DEDICATION

———>∙◦∙<———

This book is dedicated to four very special people in my life whom God has brought together, my family. First of all to my wife, Thelma, who became my lover and help-mate in 1960 and has faithfully been my encourager all these years. To our three children, Steve, Mike, and Beth who are all very special, and whom I love very much. These are the ones who, through the years in our daily Family Time, have contributed many thoughts and become an active part of the sharing of the contents of this Devotional Commentary. Of course, this family time circle has become much larger over the years as we have had the privilege of traveling and sharing these thoughts concerning God's precious Word with people around the world. I am honored that you have now become a part of this family.

ENDORSEMENTS

Lou Nicholes' commentary on the entire Bible is unique in at least three ways. First, it interprets passages from a devotional perspective. Thus, it provides not only a head knowledge of the Scriptures, but also ministers to the heart. Second, because it is the result of decades of study and personal application to his own life by the author, it contains content that has matured over the years. Third, during those years its content has been tested and proven effective in the lives of many individuals through presentations by the author.

Renald E. Showers
International Conference speaker for The Friends of Israel
Author of several books, one being "What on Earth is God Doing?"

"Daily Quiet Time" has been a trade mark for my dad as long as I can remember. Every morning at the breakfast table dad would pop the question "So what did you learn from your Quiet Time today?" This series, born out of our home, is Biblically based, life related, practical, and workable. It is not only good for your home, but for leading small groups. One taste and your hooked.

Mike Nicholes
Word of Life Missionary in South Korea
Author's second son

"For many years pastors have challenged Christian families to spend time together studying the Bible. Unfortunately, that has not happened on any wide scale. The reasons for this are many and varied, and do not need to be rehearsed here. What matters is that Lou Nicholes has done something significant to help us all in this area. He has provided an invaluable resource to help fathers and mothers take their children systematically through the Bible. I think I can safely say that there is nothing else like this book on the market today. Most of what is proposed for families tends either to be devotional or topical. Lou Nicholes takes the best of those two approaches and applies them to a systematic study of I and II Corinthians. The result is a bite-sized, user friendly, easy to read, applicational approach that covers every part of these books from the very first verse until the very last verse. You will soon discover that there are many excellent ways to use this book. You could use it to study I and II Corinthians on your own. And you could use it in a small group or a Sunday School class. But its preeminent purpose will be the one envisioned by Lou Nicholes. Families everywhere will find this an invaluable tool. From my standpoint, I not only recommend this book, I encourage Lou to continue and give us many other books of the Bible in this excellent format.

Ray Prichard
Pastor, Conference Speaker and Author
Calvary Memorial Church, Chicago, Illinois

One of the most precious memories I have growing up was coming down the stairs to see my dad sitting by himself with a Bible, a pen and a journal. He had a Quiet Time every day and passed this valuable habit to each of us. Now he is taking the best of all the nuggets he has gleaned over the past 40 plus years and is passing them on to you. Throughout his devotional commentaries you will see that from Genesis to Revelation, even in books like Leviticus, in every passage there is a practical application for us today.

Steve Nicholes
Word of Life Director in South Korea
Author's oldest son

Lou Nicholes has written what I believe will be a great help to families and to those who are interested in making the Word of God their priority. In a concise fashion he has put together a devotional commentary that will not only inspire the heart, but become a study tool for teaching. My husband, Roy and I have served side by side with Lou for many years and have watched him put into practice in his family what he has written. His faithful leadership in his own family worship has made him qualified to write so that others may be challenged and blessed.

Barbara Davoll
Children's Author
Christopher Churchmouse Series

As an elementary teacher in a Christian school, I would have my students start each day with their own Bible reading time, or Quiet Time. Gradually parents would become interested and ask about how they too could participate with their children's Bible reading program. Many parents want to be involved in the Christian education of their children but don't really know where to start. One of my earliest memories of my dad has been waking up and seeing him having his Quiet Time each day. One of his life long passions has been to help other families start their own individual and family times. This book is the culmination of all the years that my father shared his Quiet Times with our family. Having grown up in a home where we were all encouraged to share thoughts from our Quiet Time each day, I am convinced that leading your family in devotions can really change each family member's life. It can also bring your whole family closer to each other and to the Lord.

Beth Steiner
Missionary teacher to Asia
Author's daughter

PREFACE

A s you read this devotional commentary, picture yourself sitting at the breakfast table each morning with
your family, sharing something the Lord has impressed
upon each of your hearts during your Quiet Time that morning. Just think of each member of your family encouraging
and challenging each other with thoughts from the Word of
God that is fresh from your personal devotions that morning. I can honestly say that I can hardly wait to get out of
bed early each morning, splash a little water on my face and
see what the Word of God has to say to me for that day.
After jotting down a few notes about what the writer has
said, and how I plan to apply this to my life, I can hardly
wait for "Family Time" to share these thoughts the Lord has
given to me.

Actually, the thoughts expressed in this book are the
results of our family doing this each morning for many
years. We started following this format when our oldest son,
Steve, was about eight years old. Today Steve is a missionary and field director for Word of Life Fellowship in South
Korea. Our family time involved every member of our
family reading the same scripture each day, writing down a
short paragraph on an outstanding thought (if the child was

old enough to read and write), and writing another two or three lines on how he or she planned to apply this Bible principle to their life. Each child, as well as mom and dad, was given an opportunity to share these thoughts. Then we would work on a Scripture memory verse together, take prayer requests, and pray for these requests. That started over 30 years ago. Today our three children, Steve, Mike and Beth, are all out of the nest and serving the Lord in other parts of the world. Thelma and I still follow this format each morning, because it is such a blessing and has taught us so many things. Why would we want to stop?

For our personal devotions we follow a plan outlined in the Word of Life Quiet Time Diary, which was born in our office in Southern Ohio in 1967, where my wife and I began our missionary service with Word of Life Clubs over forty years ago. This devotional guide, which is now printed and distributed around the world (in different languages), was the result of a discussion with several fellow missionaries who expressed the need for something that would take us through the Bible verse by verse. After it became a habit in our own lives, we would challenge the leaders and young people we were working with to do the same.

We decided on a plan that would systematically take us through the Bible every six years. We wanted it to be in bite size pieces (just a few verses each day). In Acts 20:27 we are told not to shun the teaching of the whole council of God, so we decided to cover all sixty-six books of the Bible, asking the same two questions each day. What is the writer saying, and how do I apply this in my life? We stressed the use of the personal pronouns, I, me, and my, rather than we, us, and they, as we make this personal application each day.

The daily "Quiet Time" is great, but the most desperately needed thing in the Christian home today is the "Family Time." As I have surveyed many audiences over the years I find that less that 2% of Christian homes have a time together each day in the Word of God and prayer. Even with the ones who do, very few get every member of the family involved in sharing what God has spoken to them about that day. What a thrill it has been in our family to hear each child (who is old enough to share) tell what God has spoken to them about during their "Quiet Time."

The Results of a Survey
Taken in many Churches and Bible Conferences with thousands of Bible Believing Christians

Question #1 - How many think Christians should read their Bible and pray every day?

Answer - Almost **100%** of every audience.

Question # 2 - How many personally read their Bible and pray every day?

Answer - less than **10%** of those surveyed.

Question # 3 - How many get their family together to read their Bible and pray every day?

Answer - Always less than **2%** and sometimes almost no one.

This survey has been taken hundreds and perhaps thousands of times by the author over a period of years and every time the results have been similar.

As a result of this survey I am convinced that most Bible believing Christians would like to read their Bible and pray every day. Yet only a small percent actually do this personally and only a very few set aside a time for family devotions. The main reason they say they should but don't is is because they don't have a simple plan to follow. May the simple format of this series of Devotional Commentaries from Genesis to Revelation be an example, help and encouragement to you. You can actually use this same format to write your own commentary, get your family involved with you and experience the joy of having God speak to you on a daily basis.

INTRODUCTORY
COMMENTS

This devotional commentary is a part of a series of commentaries soon to be published, that if followed on a day by day basis will take you from the beginning of Genesis to the end of Revelation over a period of approximately six years. It is the result of this author going through the Bible book by book, passage by passage, year after year that has resulted in the content of this book which has taken on the following format.

1. Reading a selected passage and meditating on it.
2. Coming up with a one or two word topic on what has been read.
3. Recording a few thoughts concerning the content of this passage.
4. Coming up with a brief illustration to introduce these thoughts.
5. Making a personal application of what the writer has stated in this passage.
6. Selecting and memorizing one verse from the reading each week.

It is good to read the thoughts expressed in this or other commentaries, but there is no substitute for reading the Word of God each day, meditating on what the writer has to say, and writing your own commentary on what the Lord has specifically impressed on your mind. Therefore, I would highly recommend that you use the sample outline at the back of this book and write your own commentary each day. You can print out your own daily reading guide by going to www.Family-Times.net. each month. I am sure that you will be amazed at all God has to teach you through this method of having a daily quiet time. In fact, if you would like a booklet already designed for this purpose with a reading guide to follow for the year I would recommend the Word of Life Quiet Time Diary which can be purchased through Word of Life, Box 600, Schroon Lake, New York 12860.

1st

Corinthians
Problem Solving

Part of A Devotional Commentary Series

By Lou Nicholes

PASSAGE AND TOPIC INDEX

INTRODUCTION TO
I CORINTHIANS
Problem Solving

—————>•<————

- First Corinthians was written by Paul from Ephesus to a church largely made up of Gentiles.

- The city of Corinth lies fifty miles west of Athens on a narrow neck of land (four miles wide) between the Aegean and Adriatic seas. This was a crossroads for travel and commerce.

- Corinth contained a number of pagan temples, including one dedicated to Aphrodite, which was visible far out to sea. This temple was serviced by a thousand slave girls who doubled as temple prostitutes and as entertainers for the city night life.

- This, the longest of Paul's letters, deals with the quarrels and questions of the Corinthian Church. This was a gifted church but one that was carnal, worldly, and childish.

- This book gives you God's prospective on some very hot

topics as it reveals the humanity of Christians and shares how Paul deals with rumors, factions and fights in the church. Operating on the principles given in this book can have a mighty impact in today's world.

- No other epistle gives a better look at problems and conditions in an apostolic church. The wide variety of subjects discussed is easy to follow because of its logical development.

- The Gospel was first preached in Corinth by Paul on his second missionary journey. Upon arrival in the city Paul accepted the hospitality of Aquila and Priscilla who were exiled Jews from Rome. During the week he worked with them making tents (Acts 18:1-4) and on the Sabbath he reasoned with the Jews in the synagogue concerning Christ.

- Paul's letter to the Corinthians was brought about by at least two factors. First he had received word from people in the church concerning problems that included divisions in the church (1:11) and immorality (5:6-9:20). Secondly he received a letter from the assembly requesting answers to a series of questions concerning marriage, food, worship and the resurrection.

- Paul wrote this letter to address their problems, heal their divisions, and answer their questions. Paul confronted them with their sin and their need for corrective action as well as encouraging them to make a clear commitment to Christ. We could summarize his discussion into two categories; unsolicited advice (chapters 1-6&15), and solicited advice (chapters 7-14).

- An outline for the book:

    1. <u>Concern</u> (Divisions in the Church) - Chapters 1-4
    2. <u>Condemnation</u> (Disorder in the Church) - Chapters 5-6
    3. <u>Counsel</u> (Difficulties in the Church) - Chapters 7-16

I CORINTHIANS

Scripture Reading: 1:1-9

Weekly Memory verse: 1:18

Topic: Thankfulness

THOUGHTS ABOUT THE PASSAGE:

Scottish minister Alexander Whyte was known for his uplifting prayers in the pulpit. He always found something for which to be grateful. One Sunday morning the weather was so gloomy that one church member thought to himself, "Certainly the preacher won't think of anything for which to thank the Lord on a wretched day like this." Much to his surprise, however, Whyte began by praying, "We thank Thee, O God, that it is not always like this" (*Our Daily Bread, August 26, 1989*).

Paul wrote this letter to the Church in Corinth while he was visiting Ephesus during his third missionary journey (Acts 19:1-20:1). He knew the Corinthian Church well because he had spent 18 months in Corinth during his second missionary journey. Paul begins his letter by voicing his authority and explaining that he is truly an apostle (v. 1). Sosthenes may have been Paul's secretary who wrote this letter as he dictated it. He addresses this letter to the "church of God" which is at Corinth but also stresses that it is to "all who in every place call on the name of Jesus Christ our Lord" (v. 2). In other words he is making it clear this is not a private letter even though it deals with specific issues facing the

Church at Corinth.

Paul opens his letter by commending the church for its good things. Afterward he will rebuke it for the things that were wrong. He commends it and gives thanks:

1. For the grace of God given these people by Jesus Christ (v. 4).
2. For the testimony of Christ confirmed in them (v. 6)
3. That the ones to whom he is writing are expectantly waiting for the Lord's coming (v. 7).

Paul guarantees the Corinthian believers that God will consider them "blameless" when Christ returns. This guarantee was not because of their great gifts or abilities but because of what Jesus Christ had done for them.

APPLICATION:

Just as Paul begins his letter by sharing positive things, it helps for me to affirm with people what God has already accomplished in them before I am tempted to correct them.

I CORINTHIANS

Scripture Reading: 1:10-17

Weekly Memory verse: 1:18

Topic: Division

THOUGHTS ABOUT THE PASSAGE:

Being much concerned about the rise of denominations in the church, John Wesley tells of a dream he had. In the dream, he was ushered to the gates of Hell. There he asked, "Are there any Presbyterians here?" "Yes!", came the answer. Then he asked, "Are there any Baptists? Any Episcopalians? Any Methodists?" The answer was "Yes!" each time. Much distressed, Wesley was then ushered to the gates of Heaven. There he asked the same question, and the answer was "No!" "No?" To this, Wesley asked, "Who then is inside?" The answer came back, "There are only Christians here." (*Source unknown*)

Dissension in the Corinthian church was the first problem addressed by Paul. He introduces the thoughts of this passage with an appeal for unity. It seems that quarrels had split them into factions and these appears to have been *four rival parties* within the Church (vv. 11-17):

1. <u>Those who professed to follow *Paul*</u> who had founded the church.
2. <u>Those who counted themselves to be followers of *Apollos*</u>, a native of Alexandria.

3. Those who claimed to follow *Peter*, more favorable to Jewish forms and ceremonies.
4. Those who renounced all the others and claimed only *Christ*.

With the many churches and styles of worship available today, we could get caught up in this same game of "my preacher is better than yours". Paul makes it clear that God's message is much more important than any human messenger. In view of all these divisions Paul says that he is thankful that very few in Corinth were ever baptized by him (v. 14). Some speakers use a lot of impressive words but they are weak in content. Paul is stressing that solid content and practical help is what is important for the listener. The persuasive power should be in the story and not in the storyteller. Paul concludes his exhortation regarding the divisions in the church with a call to evangelize (v. 17).

APPLICATION:

I must never let my appreciation for any teacher, preacher or author cause me to follow a man rather than the message of God's Word. My allegiance must be to Jesus Christ and to the unity He desires in the body of Christ.

I CORINTHIANS

Scripture Reading: 1:18-25

Weekly Memory verse: 1:18

Topic: Knowledge

THOUGHTS ABOUT THE PASSAGE:

Knowledge is exploding at such a rate—more than 2000 pages a minute—that even Einstein couldn't keep up. In fact, if you read 24 hours a day, from age 21 to 70, and retained all you read, you would be one and a half million years behind when you finished. How can it be, in a world where half the things a man knows at 20 are no longer true at 40—and half the things he knows at 40 hadn't been discovered when he was 20? (*Campus Life, Feb., 1979*).

It is interesting to see how Paul approached this problem of division in the church. First, he pointed to the unity of Christ: there is one Saviour and one body. Then he reminded them of their baptism, a picture of their spiritual baptism into Christ's body (v. 17). The true condition of the Corinthian believers was that they were still engrossed with human, earthly wisdom. We can spend a lifetime accumulating human knowledge and still not learn how to have a personal relationship with God. The content of Paul's message in this letter was the good news of Jesus Christ, thought to be foolish because they were perpetually looking for some material sign. Many Greeks earnestly sought after wisdom through reasoning that would appeal to the intellect.

Paul illustrates his point by using an illustration from Isa. 24:19. The great stress in these verses is upon the activity of God. The emphasis of the Apostle here is not upon the act of preaching but upon the content of preaching. The message of Christ's death for sins sounds foolish to those who don't believe. Death seems like the end of the road. However, Jesus did not stay dead. His resurrection demonstrated his power even over death. This sounds so simple that many people refuse to accept it. However, the people who simply accept Christ are actually the wisest of all because they alone will live in eternity. Because the Jews were looking for power and great glory, they stumbled at the weakness of the cross. Rather than a testimony of weakness, the cross is a tremendous instrument of power! After all, the "weakness of God" (in the cross) is stronger than men (v. 25).

APPLICATION:

Paul declares that no amount of human knowledge can replace Christ's work on the cross. Lord help me to always trust in you and not in my own knowledge about you.

I CORINTHIANS

Scripture Reading: 1:26-31

Weekly Memory verse: 1:18

Topic: Nobodies

THOUGHTS ABOUT THE PASSAGE:

The saintly Scottish pastor Robert Murry McCheyne one day gave a gospel tract to a woman, and she was greatly offended. "You must not know who I am!" she said in an offended manner. "Madam," McCheyne replied, "there is coming a day of judgment, and on that day it will not matter who you are!" (*Source Unknown*).

It was Abraham Lincoln who said, "God must have loved the common people, since He made so many of them." I would modify that to say, "God must have loved the common people, since He made the way of salvation plain enough to be grasped by all." From the human viewpoint, wisdom, and people with influential background were scarce. Paul did not say- "not any", but he did say- "not many were chosen." Generally speaking, God has chosen His servants from those the world calls "foolish". It seems that he often takes those whom the world considers "nobodies" and works in their lives in such a manner as to produce heroes of faith. The reason He does this is so "no flesh should glory in His presence"(v. 29). God called them not because of what they were but in spite of what they were!

The Corinthians had a tendency to be "puffed up" with pride (vv. 4-6; 5:20). If the Lord chose many who were highly intelligent and very successful in life they might begin to think that it was by their own power that the work was being accomplished. By using "nobodies" God proves that wisdom and power are entirely His own. Therefore the Christian who boasts should never boast of himself but rather glory in the Lord (v. 31). We tend to say that because a person has natural ability, he will make a good Christian. It is not a matter of what we bring with us, but of what God puts into us; not a matter of knowledge, or of experience — all of that is of no avail. The only thing of value is the compelling purpose of God and being made one of His.

APPLICATION:

What situations can you think of where God used the weak, lowly, and despised to build His kingdom in our day? I want to be thinking of ways He has used me in the past and ways He wants to use me in the future, not because of my ability but because of my availability.

I CORINTHIANS

Scripture Reading: 2:1-5

Weekly Memory verse: 1:18

Topic: Simplicity

THOUGHTS ABOUT THE PASSAGE:

One man who was on the path of true simplicity was, according to the Talmud, a certain Rabbi Zusya. He once said, "In the coming world, they will not ask me: "Why were you not Moses?" They will ask me, "Why were you not Zusya?" (*Reader's Digest, March, 1980*).

In this passage Paul reminds the Corinthians of three things as it pertains to sharing the Gospel.

1. Our *approach* needs to be to glorify God and not our self (vv. 1-2).
2. Our *attitude* needs to be dependence on the Holy Spirit and not our ability (vv. 3-4).
3. Our *aim* needs to be to present the message and not the messenger (v. 5).

A certain church had a beautiful stained glass window behind the pulpit which depicted Jesus Christ on the Cross. The story is told that one Sunday there was a guest minister who was much smaller than the regular pastor. A little girl listened to the guest for a time, then turned to her mother and asked. "Where is the man who usually stands there so we can't see Jesus?"

From all indications Paul was a brilliant scholar and could have overwhelmed his listeners with intellectual arguments, but he shared the simple message of Jesus Christ by allowing the Holy Spirit to guide his words. Paul never tried to gather followers by using fancy words to tickle the intellectual ears of those listening to him. He was determined "not to know anything save Jesus Christ, and Him crucified"(v. 2). Of course Paul is not saying here that certain fields of human knowledge are not useful in their proper place. Instead he is determined to center his preaching around the important theme of the person and works of Jesus Christ. Some people have tried to use these verses as an excuse for not studying or preparing. Effective preaching needs much preparation but with reliance on the Holy Spirit (v. 5).

APPLICATION:

In presenting the Gospel I always want to keep the message of God's saving grace simple and not make it complicated. If a lost person stumbles over Jesus and the cross, that is their responsibility, but if they stumble over the things I may have added, it is my responsibility.

I CORINTHIANS

Scripture Reading: 2:6-9

Weekly Memory verse: 1:18

Topic: Wisdom

THOUGHTS ABOUT THE PASSAGE:

Wisdom is the reward you get for a lifetime of listening when you would have preferred to talk. You don't have to be listed in Who's Who to know what's what. Wisdom is spiritually opportunistic (Eph. 5:16–17). A wise man learns by the experience of others. An ordinary man learns by his own experience. A fool learns by nobody's experience.

In this passage we find the following characteristics of wisdom:

1. Wisdom comes from God, not man (v. 7).
2. Wisdom involves God's plan, not our plan (v. 7).
3. Wisdom results in God being glorified, not us exemplified (v. 7).
4. Wisdom is hidden from the unsaved world, but seen by the saved (v. 8).
5. Wisdom applies to the believer's life, but not to the unsaved (v. 9).

It appears that the believers in Corinth had forgotten the cost of their salvation; they had gotten their eyes off of the cross. The had been taken up with minor matters because they had lost the wonder of the greatness of God's plan for them. They needed to return to the ministry of the Holy Spirit which is covered in the next passage.

An example of this is the Gospel which is foolishness to men and can only be learned through the Holy Spirit. The rulers of this world who depend on human wisdom have no conception of God's plan on the part of God. On the contrary it was conceived in the eternal mind of God "before the ages" and carried out by His sovereign will. Originally unknown to humanity, this plan became crystal clear when Jesus rose from the dead. God's plan, however, is still hidden to unbelievers because they refuse to accept it, choose to ignore it or haven't heard about it.

APPLICATION:

It seems that the Corinthians were trying to measure "truth and success" by how powerful, influential, and articulate someone was. I must ask myself, do I ever find myself doing this same thing?

I CORINTHIANS

Scripture Reading: 2:10-16

Weekly Memory verse: 1:18

Topic: Holy Spirit

THOUGHTS ABOUT THE PASSAGE:

Have you ever heard someone say, "Don't preach doctrine to me, just give me heartwarming sermons that will encourage me!" The truth is that it is Bible doctrine that steers the spiritual ships. Unless we learn Bible doctrine we cannot know the mind of Christ. In this passage Paul deals with three vital doctrines.

1. The Doctrine of Revelation (v. 10). God has revealed Himself to us through His Word and not man's words. We can only know the mind of Christ as we search the Word of God through the *Holy Spirit.*
2. The Doctrine of Illumination (v. 11). Since the truth of God comes only from God it requires *the Spirit of God* for us to properly understand it. It is only as He shines His light on His truth that we can see and understand His truths.
3. The Doctrine of Inspiration (v. 12). The truth about God is found in the Word of God. It is important to know that in the Bible we have inspired words (John 17:8). That is why we say we believe in both the verbal and plenary inspiration of Scripture.

In verses 14 and 15 we see the contrast between the natural and the spiritual man. The unsaved man cannot understand the things of God because he does not have the Spirit of God living within. The saved person can understand because the *Holy Spirit* lives within and teaches him. The *Holy Spirit* helps us see things as they really are. A story is told of a shoe manufacturer who decided to open a market in the Congo and sent two salesmen to the undeveloped territory. One salesman cabled back: "Prospect here nil. No one wears shoes." The other salesman reported enthusiastically, "Market potential terrific! Everyone is barefooted." The Holy Spirit helps us see things as they really are from his prospective.

APPLICATION:

Am I spending enough time with Christ to know what He wants in my life? I can only know this as I spend time consistently in his presence and in His Word.

I CORINTHIANS

Scripture Reading: 3:1-9

Weekly Memory Verse: 4:2

Topic: Carnality

THOUGHTS ABOUT THE PASSAGE:

What is carnality? According to the dictionary, it means to have the nature and characteristics of the flesh (or more simply, it means "fleshly"). Sometimes it refers to the whole material part of man (1 Corinthians 15:39; Hebrews 5:7), and based on this meaning, carnal sometimes relates to material things like money (Romans 15:27) or to the opposite of our weapons of spiritual warfare (2 Corinthians 10:4). Based on this meaning of the word flesh, to be carnal means to be characterized by things that belong to the unsaved life (Ephesians 2:3). (*So Great Salvation, Charles Ryrie, Victor Books, 1989, pp. 59-60).*

Up to this point, Paul has been talking about two kinds of people in the world: those who are natural (unsaved) and those who are spiritual (saved). Now he says there are two kinds of saved people: those who are mature and those who are immature, which he calls carnal. The Corinthian Christians, who should be spiritual, were carnal and because of this, they were not able to understand the things of God. The fact that there were among them people who were filled with envying, strife and divisions was proof that they were carnal. Paul referred to them as "brethren" and babes in

41

Christ (v.1). They were truly saved but still allowing the old nature to control them.

It is not difficult to determine a believer's spiritual maturity, or immaturity, if you discover what kind of "diet" he enjoys. The "babe in Christ" lives on "Bible stories" and not Bible doctrines. If he is not hungry for the Word of God, he is either spiritually dead (not saved) or he is spiritually sick (carnal). In verses 5-9, the church is pictured as a field that ought to bear fruit. The task of the ministry is the sowing of the seed, the cultivating of the soil, the watering of the plants and the harvesting of the fruit. While men can be used to plant and cultivate things, only God can make things grow.

:APPLICATION

Carnal Christians are controlled by their own desires, while mature believers are in tune with God's desires. The question for me to ask myself is, how much influence do my desires have on my life? I need to pray that Christ will give me a spiritual appetite for His Word.

I CORINTHIANS

Scripture Reading: 3:10-15

Weekly Memory Verse: 4:2

Topic: Foundation

THOUGHTS ABOUT THE PASSAGE:

It seems that Paul is writing in this passage about the building of the Christian life. He starts out talking about the foundation, which is always the least noticed and the most important part of any building. A building is only as solid as its foundation. The foundation of a Christian's life must be Jesus Christ (v. 2). The Corinthians were emphasizing personalities when they should have been glorifying Christ. It is easy for us to have our faith in preachers and buildings rather than in Jesus Christ himself.

Paul has been the first to preach the Gospel in Corinth. He has "laid the foundation", so to speak. Now he continues the picture of constructing the building and the importance of the kind of materials that are used. There are basically two kinds of material that can be used in the superstructure of a building. The gold, silver and precious stones refer to the enduring quality of the builder's work, while the wood, hay and stubble suggests work that is temporary and of no value. These three expensive materials above suggest sound doctrines and the valueless materials are false doctrines. Two sure ways to destroy a building are to tamper with the foundation and to build with inferior materials.

A person may be able to hide the true quality of his service for Christ in this life but there is coming a time when it will be openly displayed. The time is given in the words "the day", which most Bible scholars think is the Judgment seat of Christ. Fire speaks of the righteous judgement of God. Today the work. Tomorrow the fire. If a man's work remains undamaged by the fire, he will receive rewards. If his work is consumed by the fire, everything he has devoted himself to in this life shall be suddenly swept away. We can get lazy about clearing out the weeds and thorny bushes that hinder our Christian growth but they pose a fire hazard that we should fear.

APPLICATION:

Will my Christian character stand the test? Am I building my life with things that are eternal and lasting or on things that will end with this life? Salvation depends on what Christ did for me; rewards depend on what I do for Him.

I CORINTHIANS

Scripture Reading: 3:16-23

Weekly Memory Verse: 4:2

Topic: Wisdom

THOUGHTS ABOUT THE PASSAGE:

Just as our bodies are the temple of the Holy Spirit, the local church or Christian community is God's temple. In verses 16-17, Paul is warning the Corinthian believers that if they use cheap materials in building the temple, God will destroy it. The builder will see the loss of his labor, but he himself will be saved, like a burning stick that is snatched from the fire.

In verses 18-23 Paul continues to challenge his Corinthian brothers and sisters in Christ about their love of human wisdom. Paul carefully contrasts the wisdom of this world in verses 18-20 with the wisdom of God in verses 21-23. What these Corinthian Christians have done in pretending to be wise by the standards of the world is making them look foolish in the eyes of God. Paul says, "You must stop exalting men, put an end to divisions, deny any wisdom that you think you have, and instead embrace God's wisdom and the tremendous riches and blessings."

Paul was not telling the Corinthian believers to neglect the pursuit of knowledge, but he was warning them that so-called worldly wisdom is not wisdom at all. The Corinthians were using worldly wisdom to evaluate their leaders and teachers. *They were more concerned about the presentation of the message than they were about its content.* The world depends on education and the promotion of important people. What the Christian needs to depend on is prayer and the Holy Spirit's power with humility, sacrifice and service. Most of the leaders in the early church were ordinary men who had no special education.

Perhaps we cannot help but have personal preferences when it comes to the way different men minister the Word of God. But we must not allow these personal preferences to divide us like the Corinthians did. In fact, the preacher or teacher I enjoy the least may be the one I need the most. Paul admonishes us to get our eyes off men and keep them on Christ.

APPLICATION:

My ministry or work will never go any deeper than I have gone myself. It is useless to ask God to work through me until He has first of all worked in me. I have a choice of seeking worldly wisdom or the wisdom that only God can give me.

I CORINTHIANS

Scripture Reading: 4:1-5

Weekly Memory Verse: 4:2

Topic: Steward

THOUGHTS ABOUT THE PASSAGE:

St. Augustine wrote
Where your pleasure is, there is your treasure.
Where your treasure is, there is your heart.
Where your heart is, there is your happiness.
(*In Who Said That by George Sweeting*)

In this chapter, Paul presents three characteristics of a true minister of Jesus Christ:

1. He is to be a faithful steward (vv.1-5).

    A steward is one who takes care of another person's affairs but owns nothing himself. In today's world he might be called a manager. It is not *my* money (He is letting me handle it for a while), *my* church (He is just giving me a place to serve Him), or *my* children (They are on loan to us for a few years so that we can train them). A true minister is to be one who shares God's wealth with the family of God. He may not please the members of his household. His responsibility is to be faithful to his master. He is to do what his master tells him to do.

47

Paul brings to our attention three judgments in the life of a steward.

a. <u>What do you think of me</u>? (v. 3a). Paul says that it doesn't matter what the Corinthians may think of him. His Master's judgment is what counts.
b. <u>What do I think of me</u>? (vv. 3b-4a). It is not of supreme importance what a person thinks of himself. It is very difficult for us to judge ourselves. In fact there is a fine line between a clear conscience and a self-righteous attitude.
c. <u>What does God think of me</u>? (v. 4b). The final and proper judge is the Lord. When He comes He will judge the acts and motives of all Christians. Then each person shall have the praise which is rightly due him.

APPLICATION:

It is very tempting for me to judge fellow Christians by evaluating whether or not they are good followers of Christ. I must remember that it is only God who knows a person's heart, and He is the only one who has the right to judge.

I CORINTHIANS

Scripture Reading: 4:6-13

Weekly Memory Verse: 4:2

Topic: Humility

THOUGHTS ABOUT THE PASSAGE:

A well-known Christian businessman who was visiting a church was asked to give his testimony. He said, "I have a fine family, a large house, a successful business, and a good reputation. I have plenty of money so I can support some Christian ministries very generously. Many organizations want me on their board of directors. I have good health and almost unlimited opportunities. What more could I ask from God?" As he paused for effect, a voice shouted from the back of the auditorium, "How about asking Him for a good dose of humility?" (*Source unknown*)

 2. He is to be a humble example (vv. 6-13).

   The Corinthians were wise in their own eyes, but they were actually fools in the sight of God. Paul asks three pointed questions that puncture the bubble of the Corinthian pride (v. 7).

   a. For who maketh thee to differ? In other words, who regards you as superior? There was no room for pride and self-conceit when everything they were they owed to God.

49

b. <u>What has thou received?</u> Everything they had, including their gifts in the ministry were given them by God. To take any credit personally was an insult to Him.

c. <u>Why doest thou glory?</u> John the Baptist said "a man can receive nothing, except it be given him from Heaven...He (Christ) must increase, but I must decrease" (John 3:27,30).

Apparently trying to humble the Corinthians, Paul makes a series of contrasts. He said, "You are trying to act as kings when we are prisoners subject to death" (vv. 7-9). He said, "you want people to see you as strong men when in ourselves we are weak" (v. 10). Finally He said, "you want the honor that comes from men instead of being associated with us and ready for suffering" (vv. 11-13).

APPLICATION:

Lord, help me not to try to take the credit for things you do for me, give to me or allow me to accomplish.

I CORINTHIANS

Scripture Reading: 4:14-21

Weekly Memory Verse: 4:2

Topic: Gentleness

THOUGHTS ABOUT THE PASSAGE:

Sometimes in our zeal to clean up our own lives or the lives of others, we unfortunately use "killer soaps"—condemnation, criticism, nagging, fits of temper. We think we're doing right, but our harsh, self-righteous treatment is more than they can bear. - (*Source unknown*)

3. <u>He is a tender father</u> (vv. 14-21). The Corinthians were Paul's beloved children in the faith and he talks to them as a loving father would to his wayward children. Whenever we share the Gospel with someone and have the joy of leading them to faith in Christ, we become a "spiritual parent" in his life. Paul was an example to his spiritual family. He was also a good teacher. It takes both example and instruction to bring a child to maturity. He realized that if all he did was expose his readers to open shame, he would only provoke them. He was not like the modern mother who shouts at her disobedient child, "This is the last time I'm going to tell you!" He knew that he had to discipline them.

He would have preferred to come to them in meekness and

deal with their sins in a gentle manner, but their own attitude made this difficult. He was not interested in making them cringe before him, but in correcting them and offering them a chance to respond and be restored. He ends by saying, "Shall I come unto you with a rod or in love?" (v. 21). It is all up to them. Paul is giving instruction on how to handle personal relationships:

a. <u>Proclaim confidence</u> - We must convey some sense of confidence and love first.
b. <u>Present a model</u> - People will always follow what you do and not what you say.
c. <u>Preserve liberty</u> - Admonish, not command. Give liberty for making a choice.
d. <u>Project reality</u> - Talk is cheap but change results in fruit. Walk your talk!

APPLICATION:

There is a big difference between knowing the right words and living them out. I need to let my life show that God's power is really working in me. What am I doing, where is my fruit, and what are the results of the ministry God has entrusted me with?

I CORINTHIANS

Scripture Reading: 5:1-13

Weekly Memory Verse: 4:2

Topic: Church Discipline

THOUGHTS ABOUT THE PASSAGE:

A report came to Paul of a serious sin in the church at
Corinth that was not being dealt with. The issue concerned a
Corinthian church member who was carrying on an incestu-
ous affair with his stepmother. This kind of relationship was
prohibited in the Old Testament (Lev. 18:8) and in Roman
law. Paul gives them three specific instructions to follow as
a church:

1. Mourn over the sin (vv. 1-2). Paul states that even
    godless, unsaved Gentiles would turn in shame from
    such a sin. Instead of mourning, the church members
    at Corinth were boasting that their church was so
    "broad-minded" that even fornicators could still be
    members in good standing. The response should
    have been grief for this brother, confronting him
    with his sin and exercising church discipline.
2. Judge the sin (vv. 3-5). By the authority vested in
    him as an apostle, Paul passed judgment on the
    offender and asked that they take action by calling a
    meeting and expelling him from the church, accord-
    ing to divine instructions (Matthew 18:15-20). Of
    course this was to be done in love and with the

purpose of restoration.
3. <u>Purge the sin</u> (vv. 6-13). Paul left no doubt that a church member committing open sin should be removed from the fellowship of the assembly. The sinning church member was like a piece of yeast; he was defiling the whole congregation. This should not be applied to those outside the church as such a stand would necessitate leaving this world.

You may be wondering how things worked out in Corinth. Let's look to 2 Corinthians 2:4-8 for the answer. This whole matter of church discipline tells us something about the seriousness of sin. Sin in the church is so serious that Paul tells the Corinthians, "If this man will not repent of his sin, then deliver him unto Satan." That's pretty serious!

APPLICATION:

The Bible instructs us not to criticize people by gossiping or making rash judgments but, at the same time, we are admonished to judge and deal with sin in our lives and the lives of others. Lord, help me to see myself as I really am and be more concerned about any sin that may be in my life than that in the lives of others.

I CORINTHIANS

Scripture Reading: 6:1-11

Weekly Memory Verse: 6:19-20

Topic: Lawsuits

THOUGHTS ABOUT THE PASSAGE:

In this chapter Paul shifts to another problem within the Corinthian church. The same failure of dealing with the immoral brother was also found in cases of personal disputes between church members. It is evident in this chapter that Paul is disturbed and can hardly believe that members of the Corinthian church are bringing lawsuits against each other. See John 5:22 and Revelation 3:21 for more on judging the world. Judging angels is mentioned in II Peter 2:4 and Jude 6.

He says this is a tragedy for at least three reasons:

1. The believers were presenting a poor testimony to the unsaved community (vv. 2,6).
2. They were asking pagan judges to settle problems that they ought to be able to settle with the Lord's wisdom (vv. 3-4).
3. It was a no win situation, as the members suing each other had already lost. Even if some of them won their cases, they had created a far greater loss in their disobedience to the Word of God.

It would seem that there were some in the Corinthian church who had professed Christianity as a system of doctrine, but not as a rule of life. Paul reminds them that they have been bought with a price (the precious blood of Christ) and set apart to do God's special work. In such an exalted position, it seems incredible that they would find it necessary to go before an inferior human court to arbitrate their disputes (v. 11).

In the last two verses of this chapter Paul breaks out into a terrible catalogue of sins that is a grim commentary on the wicked civilization in which the Corinthian Church was growing up. The proof of Christianity lay in the power of the gospel. It could take the dregs of humanity and make them into men. It can take men lost to shame and make them sons of God.

APPLICATION:

God expects his followers in any age to have high standards. I should periodically review a list of the Biblical standards that I have for myself and discuss them with my family.

I CORINTHIANS

Scripture Reading: 6:12-20

Weekly Memory Verse: 6:19-20

Topic: Purity

THOUGHTS ABOUT THE PASSAGE:

In these verses, the apostle once more takes up the question of sexual immorality, a sin that was prevalent in Corinth. The temple of the love goddess, Aphrodite, was there. It employed more than a thousand prostitutes and sex was part of the worship ritual. In other words Corinth was a morally bankrupt city. Paul, who founded the church in Corinth was distressed by this situation and gives six reasons why *we must flee from sexual immorality* to stay sexually pure:

1. Because our bodies (which here refers to our total person) were designed and created for a relationship with the Lord and His Service "Now the body is not for fornication, but for the Lord, and the Lord for the body" (v. 13).
2. Because there is a future (resurrection) for these bodies of ours. "And God hath raised up the Lord, and will also raise up us by His own power" (v. 14).
3. Because our bodies are members of Christ, and we are one with Him in spirit (vv. 15-17). As ones whose bodies are one with Christ, sexually defiling ourselves is not an option.
4. Because such acts cause us great personal harm,

when we sin against our own bodies. "Every sin that a man doeth is without the body; but he that committeth fornication sinneth against his own body" (v. 18).

5. Because our body is the temple of the Holy Spirit. "What! know ye not that your body is the temple of the Holy Spirit which is in you?" (v. 19).

6. Because our body is not our own. "For ye are bought with a price: therefore glorify God in your body, and in your spirit, which are God's" (v. 20).

APPLICATION:

I must never think that I can handle in my own strength the temptations that are sure to come my way. I need to have standards in my life that will help build a hedge of protection around me. For instance, when I started out in the youth ministry I promised God that I would never allow myself to be alone in a car or isolated spot with a person of the opposite sex. Lord, hold me to it! I know that better men than me have fallen because they didn't have a hedge.

I CORINTHIANS

Scripture Reading: 7:1-9

Weekly Memory Verse: 6:19-20

Topic: Singleness

THOUGHTS ABOUT THE PASSAGE:

Statistics tell us that 37% of adults over 18 are single. During the average person's lifetime, a significant portion of their life will be spent single. Typically the first 25 years of life and perhaps the last 10-15 years will be spent as a single person.

As you read this chapter, keep in mind that Paul is replying to definite questions and not bringing an exhaustive study on marriage. This is more completely covered in Ephesians, Colossians and the letters to Timothy. Warren Wiersbe in his book, "Be Wise," states that Paul's counsel here is basically to three different groups of believers: (1) Christians who are married to Christians - (vv. 1-11), (2) Christians who are married to non-Christians (vv. 12-24), and un-married Christians (vv. 25-40).

1. <u>Christians who are married to Christians</u> (vv. 1-11). Apparently one of the questions the church asked Paul was, "Is remaining unmarried more spiritual than marriage?" Not only did the church ask about singleness but they also asked about living with their spouse.

a. <u>It is not wrong for a man not to marry</u> (v. 1,7).
b. <u>Singleness is permitted but it is not commanded</u> (v. 6). It seems there was a reactionary group in the church who were recommending singleness as desirable, if not obligatory, for all believers.
c. <u>Not everyone has the gift of remaining single</u> (vv. 7-8). Not every person is gifted with the gift of singleness. Paul apparently had the gift.
d. <u>Those who are married are not to live as singles</u> (vv. 1-7). In the Corinthian church there was a group of marrieds who thought themselves more spiritual if they refrained from sexual relations with their spouses.

APPLICATION;

The Lord has said that I am to be content in whatever situation I find myself in. I am so thankful for the wonderful wife and family he has given me for many years. Thank you, Lord!

I CORINTHIANS

Scripture Reading: 7:10-24

Weekly Memory Verse: 6:19-20

Topic: Divorce

THOUGHTS ABOUT THE PASSAGE:

Howard Hendricks was speaking at a conference in Dallas, and asked the question of the audience of 2000, "Do you know someone who is perfect?" He was about to go on, when he noticed a lone hand raised in the back of the auditorium. Hendricks asked, "Are you perfect, or do you know someone who is?" The man replied, "Oh, no, I'm not perfect. But as far as I can tell, my wife's first husband was." It is easier in these United States to walk away from a marriage than from a commitment to purchase a used car. (*Time, September, 1993, quote from a professor at George Washington University School of Law*).

In the previous passage it has been clear that the instructions were for cases where both the husband and wife were Christians. Now the apostle speaks of the situation where, after marriage one spouse becomes saved and the other is not. The question is asked, does this make it permissible for the converted one to leave the unconverted? Paul answers with an absolute no.

2.   <u>Christians who are married to non-Christians</u> (vv. 12-24). Although it is an act of disobedience for a

Christian to knowingly marry an unsaved person (II Cor. 6:14), it appears some of the members of the Corinthian church were saved after they had been married, but their mates had not been converted. Because of the desire to serve Christ, some people in the Corinthian church thought they ought to divorce their heathen spouses. He makes it plain that there is no reason why a believer should put away his unbelieving spouse. Paul like Jesus believed that marriage was permanent (vv. 12-14). When it says, in verse 15, that he "is not under bondage," it means he is not obligated to try to prevent the unsaved spouse from leaving, but this does not give freedom for remarriage. Paul's command about the permanence of marriage (vv. 10-11) comes from the Old Testament (Gen. 2:24) and from Jesus (Mark 10:2-12). The believers should continue to live in the marriage union if the other partner is willing to do so.

APPLICATION:

Whatever my circumstance in life may be, it should have no bearing on whether or not I live for Christ. Pleasing God and living for Him should be my number one goal in life.

I CORINTHIANS

Scripture Reading: 7:25-40

Weekly Memory Verse: 6:19-20

Topic: Marriage

THOUGHTS ABOUT THE PASSAGE:

3. <u>Unmarried Christians</u> (vv. 25-40). The question was, "Must a Christian get married?" The extreme Jewish view was that it was a sin if a man reached twenty years of age without being married. Paul points out that the single man or woman has greater freedom to serve the Lord.

Paul had already addressed a brief word to this group in the beginning part of this chapter, but in this closing section he goes into greater detail. He addresses this passage primarily to the parents of girls who were of marriage age. He asks them to consider several factors when they make their decision about whether to marry or not to marry.

4. <u>Consider the present circumstances</u> (vv. 25-31). It was a time of distress (v. 26) when the world was going through change (v. 31). Those who marry must be ready to accept the trials that will accompany it (v. 28).

5. <u>Face the responsibilities honestly</u> (vv. 32-35). There is no need to rush into marriage and create more problems. Marriage requires a measure of maturity,

and age is no guarantee of maturity. As much as possible, we should live unhindered by the cares of this world, not getting involved with burdensome mortgages, investments or debts that will keep us from doing God's work.

6. <u>Be aware that each situation is unique</u> (vv. 36-38). Because each situation is unique, parents and children must seek the Lord's will. It takes more than two Christian people to make a happy marriage. Marriage does not hold two people together but commitment does.

7. <u>Remember that marriage is for life</u> (vv. 39-40). It is God's will that marriage is a lifetime commitment. There is no place for a "trial marriage" and thinking that if things don't work out we can always get a divorce.

APPLICATION:

Paul is saying that I should be content in the stage of life that I'm presently in, whether I'm married or single. I should never be so concerned about what I could be doing for God somewhere else that I miss great opportunities right where I am.

I CORINTHIANS

Scripture Reading: 8:1-6

Weekly Memory Verse: 6:19-20

Topic: Stumbling block

THOUGHTS ABOUT THE PASSAGE:

Charles Spurgeon frequently visited Monaco. which had been a gambling resort for years. Spurgeon, of course, was not a gambler, but he enjoyed visiting the grounds of the Casino of Monte Carlo and walking through its lavish gardens. Spurgeon thought the gardens were some of the most beautiful in the world. One day after a conversation with a friend, Spurgeon determined that he would never go there again. The owner of the casino had said to Spurgeon's friend, "You hardly ever visit my gardens anymore." Spurgeon's friend replied that since he didn't gamble it would not be fair of him to continue to enjoy the beautiful gardens without making some contribution to the casino. The owner encouraged the friend to continue visiting because he would lose customers if the friend quit visiting the gardens. He said, "There are many people who don't intend to gamble in the casino who feel quite comfortable visiting the gardens. Then, from the gardens, it is but a short distance to the gambling tables. You see, when you visit my gardens, you attract other people who eventually become my gambling customers." (*Source Unknown*)

Paul answers one of the most controversial subjects that the

Corinthians had asked in their letter. "Is it a sin for Christians to eat meat that has been sacrificed to idols?" The basic principle involved is, "What is the proper Christian attitude toward things that are harmless in themselves but have an evil connotation to others?" Some of the Christians, while knowing theoretically that an idol was nothing, were unable to break away from old associations in which they thought of these idols as evil deities. In answer to this, Paul says, "Knowledge must be balanced by love" (v. 1-3). Among the Corinthian Christians there evidently was considerable difference of opinion as to whether believers should or should not partake of such meat. Some of the Christians displayed a know-it-all attitude by saying there was nothing wrong with eating the meat offered to idols, and those who refused to eat it were just ignorant. Instead of building up the weak saints, the strong Christians were only puffing themselves up. Paul says that if it causes his brother to stumble, he is willing to give up not just meat offered to idols, but meat itself (v. 13).

APPLICATION:

My Christian standard should be not only to totally abstain from that which is evil, but also to refrain from doing anything that might be a stumbling block to others.

I CORINTHIANS

Scripture Reading: 8:7-13

Weekly Memory Verse: 6:19-20

Topic: Conscience

THOUGHTS ABOUT THE PASSAGE:

A man consulted a doctor, "I've been misbehaving, Doc, and my conscience is troubling me," he complained. "And you want something that will strengthen your willpower?" asked the doctor. "Well, no," said the fellow. "I was thinking of something that would weaken my conscience." (*Bits & Pieces, May 27, 1993, Page 21*).

The word conscience is used 32 times in the New Testament and it plays a big part in what we do or what we do not do in life. It is that part of us that either approves or condemns our actions. It is not necessarily governed by law but depends on knowledge. Therefore, the more spiritual knowledge we have and act upon, the stronger the conscience will become. The conscience of a weak Christian is easily defiled (v. 7), wounded (v. 12), and offended (v. 13).

Some who have not been a Christian for very long may have a <u>weak</u> <u>conscience</u> because they have not had time to grow. Others do not grow because they ignore their Bibles and opportunities to learn under sound teaching. They do not have a plan for reading their Bible and praying each day, no matter how long they have been a Christian. However, some remain weak because they are afraid of the freedom they have in Christ. Warren Wiersbe says, "They are like a child old enough to go to school, but are afraid to leave home and must be taken to school each day by their mother."

It seems that Paul may have been faced with a combination of both of the above. As ridiculous as it may seem, there were some who still thought that heathen gods were real beings. The big question was how the stronger brothers should react to this. Paul makes it plain that if the weaker brother thinks something is wrong and you cause him to go against his conscience and do it, that is sin (v. 12). Therefore the stronger brother must be willing to limit himself for the sake of the weaker. It is love and not knowledge that motivates a person to do this. Where knowledge is balanced by love, the strong Christian will have a ministry to the weak Christian.

APPLICATION:

It has been said, "Knowledge must be mixed with love, otherwise the saints will end up with big heads instead of enlarged hearts." Lord help me to have a big heart and not a big head.

I CORINTHIANS

Scripture Reading: 9:1-10

Weekly Memory Verse: 10:13

Topic: Support

THOUGHTS ABOUT THE PASSAGE:

In the summer of 1986, two ships collided in the Black Sea off the coast of Russia. Hundreds of passengers died as they were hurled into the icy waters below. News of the disaster was further darkened when an investigation revealed the cause of the accident. It wasn't a technology problem like radar malfunction—or even thick fog. The cause was human stubbornness. Each captain was aware of the other ship's presence nearby. Both could have steered clear, but according to news reports, neither captain wanted to give way to the other. Each was too proud to yield first. By the time they came to their senses, it was too late. (*Closer Walk, December, 1991*).

In chapter nine Paul deals with those who invoke the principle of Christian liberty. He points out that there are many things that he is free to do but which he abstains from doing for the sake of the Church. He is well aware of Christian freedom, but equally aware of Christian responsibility.
Paul uses himself as an illustration of giving up personal rights. He has the right to hospitality, to be married, and to be paid for his work (vv. 4-5). But he willingly gave up these rights to win people to Christ.

Jesus said that workers deserve their wages (Lk 10:7). Paul echoes this thought and urges the church to be sure to pay their Christian workers. Although Paul himself had not taken any money from the Corinthians, he defends his right and that of other Christian ministers to receive financial support from those to whom they minister. He compares the minister with a soldier, a vinedresser, and a shepherd (v. 7). Such are not expected to support themselves by some outside work. If any should say that these are just human illustrations, and that Paul is speaking as a man, he says that the law of God teaches the same principle. Deuteronomy 25:4 is quoted, indicating that the ox which treaded out the grain was not to be muzzled. In other words, the true Christian minister should be supported by the people to whom he ministers.

APPLICATION:

It is our duty to see that those who serve us in the ministry are fairly and adequately taken care of. Lord, help me to be a person who is looking for ways I can support missionaries and good Bible teaching ministries around the world.

I CORINTHIANS

Scripture Reading: 9:11-18

Weekly Memory Verse: 10:13

Topic: Motives

THOUGHTS ABOUT THE PASSAGE:

Different people serve God for different reasons. We know that there are definitely some reasons for serving God that are unacceptable. Jesus made it clear that striving for position and popularity are unacceptable motives for ministry. Greed is also an unacceptable motive for serving God, "not greedy for money, but eager to serve". The question is, what are acceptable motives for serving our Lord? In verses 16-17 Paul gives us three levels of motivation for serving the Lord. Not all levels are equal as being acceptable before God but each is legitimate according to Paul. In this passage Paul shares three motives for serving the Lord:

1. Fear of disobedience (v. 16) - Paul says that there are no grounds for boasting in the fact that he is a preacher of the gospel. His preaching came about not because of his choice initially but he says, "necessity is laid upon me". Here he is obviously speaking of God's call upon his life on the road to Damascus. Fear is the lowest level of motivation, but we should tremble at the thought of disobeying God's voice.
2. A sense of duty (v. 17) - There is something to be

said for duty. While this is not the highest motive, and the most desirable motive for service to Christ, it is an acceptable motive. Sometimes it's simply our duty to God that keeps us going when we don't feel like it. Jesus dreaded the cross in Gethsemane, but he remained loyal to the Father and His plan, and submitted His human will to that of the Father. Remember he "endured" the cross. Sometimes we too must "endure" when serving simply because God has entrusted us with a responsibility.

3. Willing service (v. 17) - This is the highest and holiest motive for serving our Saviour. Paul said, "If I do this thing willingly, I have a reward." To serve God willingly is to serve Him because we love Him. Those who serve in this manner have been so touched and moved by the Love of God that their will is meshed with His.

APPLICATION:

It is my desire to serve the Lord with His Spirit of Love and with the highest of motives. But may I not forget the other two motives when love fails.

I CORINTHIANS

Scripture Reading: 9:19-23

Weekly Memory Verse: 10:13

Topic: Adaptability

THOUGHTS ABOUT THE PASSAGE:

For eighteen fruitful years, Dr. H.A. Ironside pastored the Moody Church in Chicago. When he got ready to take the offering, he would often say, "We ask God's people to give generously. If you are not a believer in Jesus Christ, we do not ask you to give. We have a gift for you - eternal life through faith in Christ!" (*Source Unknown*)

The sole reward that Paul desired was to be able to preach "the gospel of Christ without charge." Someone might ask the question, with all the freedom in the world open to him, why did the apostle Paul restrict himself so severely? The answer is "that I might gain the more." (v. 19) In other words, his greatest interest was to preach the gospel and win men and women to Jesus Christ. He summarizes his guiding principle in the words, "I am made all things to all men, that I might by all means save some" (v. 22). In order to better accomplish his purpose, he was willing to adapt himself to the people with whom he was dealing. To the Jew he became as a Jew; to the Gentiles, as one of them. Acts 13 and 14 provide excellent illustrations of this principle.

Of course the apostle does not at all mean that he compromised the essentials of the Word of God, nor does he mean that he stooped to any evil deed. We must keep in mind that Paul was not a chameleon who changed his message and his methods with each new situation. Neither was he a compromiser who adjusted his message to please his audience. He was a Jew who had a great burden for his own people (Rom. 9:1-3), but also a special calling to minister to Gentiles (Eph 3:8).

What Paul does mean is that whether dealing with men under the law (Jews) or without law (Gentiles) he adapted himself to their condition. He had the right to eat whatever pleased him, but he gave up that right so that he might win the Jews. At the same time he respected the law but set the law aside so that he might reach the lost Gentiles.

APPLICATION:

I must never compromise the gospel but I want to be a person who is willing to change the way I do things in order to reach more people for Him. This may involve changing the way I spend my time or the methods I use doing it.

I CORINTHIANS

Scripture Reading: 9:24-27

Weekly Memory Verse: 10:13

Topic: Discipline

THOUGHTS ABOUT THE PASSAGE:

Paul continues to deal with the subject of Christian liberty as he uses the illustration of an athlete. The Corinthians would have been very familiar with the Greek Olympic games as well as their Isthmian games, which were held on alternate summers within the vicinity of Corinth. He says that one of the most important rules in a race is that all participants run but only one receives the prize (v.24). In the Christian life, all can win an incorruptible crown, while in an earthly contest the prize is merely "a corruptible crown." (v. 25)

An athlete must be disciplined if he is to win the prize. If he intends to win the crown, he restricts himself in all things; his diet, his activities, his associations, and probably even his friendships. He abstains from all practices which might hinder him from winning the race, even though these things might be harmless in themselves.

One day every believer will stand before the Judgement Seat of Christ. We will receive a crown if we have disciplined our bodies to serve the Lord and win the lost to Christ. This means keeping our bodies under control and our eyes on the goal. The thing that Paul feared most was that he might get into such a spiritual condition that he would lose the reward that he so much desired of the Lord Jesus Christ. (v. 27)

This passage can be summarized as follows:

1. This race of life is a battle.
2. To win the battle the race demands discipline.
3. We need to keep our eye on the goal and not look at others in the grandstands.
4. We need to know the value of our goal, which is pleasing Christ.
5. We cannot serve others until we have mastered ourselves.

APPLICATION:

My desire is that I will be disciplined in my life to the point that I will never stray off course to the very end. My prayer is that I might finish well.

I CORINTHIANS

Scripture Reading: 10:1-5

Weekly Memory Verse: 10:13

Topic: Immaturity

THOUGHTS ABOUT THE PASSAGE:

A man had a sign on his door which said, "Lead me not into temptation, I can find it myself."

In this chapter Paul uses Israel as an example of spiritual immaturity, which is shown in their overconfidence and lack of self discipline. They never seem to come to the place in their Christian walk where they are free from temptation. Paul reminded the experienced believers not to become over-confident in their ability to withstand temptation. He gives real and graphic examples from the Old Testament of people who started well but, through self-indulgence and lack of self-discipline, lost their reward. The five "alls" in verses 1-4 emphasize the five downward steps in verses 5-10.

The five "alls":

1. "under the cloud" (v. 1) - divine guidance
2. "passed through the sea" (v. 1) - divine deliverance
3. "baptized unto Moses" (v. 2) - divine leadership
4. "eat the same spiritual meat" (v. 3) - divine provision
5. "drink the same spiritual drink" (v. 4) - divine intervention

Israel had the cloud of God's presence and guidance. When the people passed through the Red Sea they were freed of the enslavements of Egypt, which is a symbol of the world. God gave Israel Moses, the leader it needed to reach the promised land. Israel partook of the food and water that God provided. He took care of their day to day necessities. It was Jesus, our Lord and Savior, who was guiding and providing for Israel through its wilderness journey toward the promised land. However, what happened to most of the people is tragic. There were over two million Jews who stepped out to follow God to the promised land but only two made it.

Application:

Thank you, Lord, for giving to me an escape route from any temptation that may come my way. When I am tempted, help me to not want to go the way of the flesh, but your way.

I CORINTHIANS

Scripture Reading: 10:6-13

Weekly Memory Verse: 10:13

Topic: Temptation

THOUGHTS ABOUT THE PASSAGE:

Paul points out that the Corinthian church was guilty of the same sins that the Jews committed.

A. **Five downward steps of temptation for the Israelites:**

1. They lusted after evil things - (v. 6, Num. 11:4) They wanted the things back in Egypt.
2. They worshiped idols - (v. 7, Ex. 32:6) - The golden calf worshiped in the wilderness.
3. They committed immorality - (v. 8, Num. 25:1-9) - Baal worship and sexual immorality.
4. They tested God's patience - (v. 9, Num. 21:6) - Israelites spoke against God and Moses.
5. They murmured - (v. 10, Num. 16:41-49) - Complained about Moses and Aaron.

B. **Three conclusions about temptation in verse 13:**

1. Temptation will come. It is not designed to make us fall but to make us stronger.
2. Temptation comes to everyone. Don't feel that you have been singled out.

79

3. <u>Temptation can be resisted</u>. God will help you resist it.

C. Five ways God will help you resist temptation:

1. <u>Recognize</u> the people and situation that give you trouble.
2. <u>Run</u> from anything that you know is wrong.
3. <u>Choose</u> to do what is right.
4. <u>Pray</u> for God's help.
5. <u>Seek</u> for friends who can help you.

All of these things which happened to the Israelites in the Old Testament were not recorded just to give us some interesting historical information, but to admonish us to have victory in our lives.

APPLICATION:

God promises that He will not permit me to be swept away by some overpowering temptation.

I CORINTHIANS

Scripture Reading: 10:14-22

Weekly Memory Verse: 10:13

Topic: Offensive

THOUGHTS ABOUT THE PASSAGE

Paul returns to the subject with which this letter began - the eating of meat offered to idols. In expressing their Christian liberty, some of the Corinthians were living dangerously close to idolatry. Paul says that it is true that an idol is nothing, but the ones behind every idol are very real (v. 20). What he was concerned about was that behind the idols are evil spirits. To attend a heathen feast resulted in their having fellowship with demons. It is not possible to be in fellowship with the Lord and demons at the same time.

In verses 14-30 Paul gives advice in three areas:

1. Concerning meat in the temple. (vv. 14-22)
2. Concerning meat in the marketplace. (vv. 25,26)
3. Concerning meat in the home. (vv. 27-30)

His advice on today's passage concerning the meat offered to idols in the temple is that even though there is freedom to eat it, they needed to be careful that they didn't participate with demons. He compares the worship at the Lord's Supper and the unity of the Christians in their participation in the blood of Christ and in the body of Christ. The one loaf of bread where all partake pictures this unity.

Paul's point in these verses about the Lord's Supper was like that made earlier (5:6-8). The collective worship of Christians at the Lord's Supper expressed the unity among the members as they participated (fellowshiped in the blood of Christ and in the body of Christ). The one loaf of bread, of which all partake, pictured their unity as members of the one body of Christ. Likewise in the worship in the temple, the participants identified with what was sacrificed and with each other.

APPLICATION:

Even though I have liberty to eat anything, I need to be careful when I am in other countries not to eat things and do things that will offend the Christians.

I CORINTHIANS

Scripture Reading: 10:23-33

Weekly Memory Verse: 10:13

Topic: Christian Liberty

THOUGHTS ABOUT THE PASSAGE:

A prayer before the U.S. Senate. "Lord Jesus, thou who art the way, the truth, and the life; hear us as we pray for the truth that shall make all free. Teach us that liberty is not only to be loved but also to be lived. Liberty is too precious a thing to be buried in books. It costs too much to be hoarded. Help us see that our liberty is not the right to do as we please, but the opportunity to please to do what is right." (*By Peter Marshall*).

Sometimes its hard to know when to defer to the weaker brother. Paul gives a simple rule of thumb to help in making that decision. He states that while we have freedom in Christ, we shouldn't exercise our freedom at the cost of hurting a Christian brother or sister. From verse 23-33 Paul lays down the principles which govern Christian liberty:

1. The principle of expedience - We must not judge our actions simply by whether it is lawful but whether it causes a brother to stumble (v. 23). We can never glorify God by causing another Christian to stumble.
2. The principle of edification - If what I do brings me into subjection rather than helping me glorify Christ,

then I need to avoid it (v. 23).

3. The principle of conscience - Since there is nothing wrong with eating meat offered to idols, you don't need to ask questions but just eat it (v. 27). However, if a weaker brother tells you it has been offered to idols and thinks it is wrong, you should not eat it (v. 28).

4. The principle of evangelism - Is my participation going to hinder or help people to come to a saving knowledge of Christ (v. 33)? We must not live to seek our own benefit, but also the benefit of others, that they might be saved.

Freedom comes from knowledge. "And ye shall know the truth, and the truth shall make you free" (Jn 8:32). However, with freedom comes responsibility, just like driving my car on the road.

APPLICATION:

I should never live my life by seeing how near to sin I can get without being contaminated, but rather how far I can stay away from it.

I CORINTHIANS

Scripture Reading: 11:1-16

Weekly Memory Verse: 11:3

Topic: Respect

THOUGHTS ABOUT THE PASSAGE:

One of the biggest problems in the Corinthian church was improper conduct in the public meetings. Two of the issues Paul deals with in this chapter are women praying and prophesying, and instructions regarding the Lord's Supper. The topic of head coverings (vv. 4-7) is not one of the fundamentals of the faith but deals with the matter of obedience. One pastor said, "This may not be a **camel** but it is a fairly good sized **gnat** we dare not ignore." Paul uses the hair as a symbol to teach respect and responsibility. We all have our biases and the culture in which we have grown up can affect our view of this subject. We should be very careful about making this a proof text for views which are contradicted elsewhere in Scripture.

The following are some things to consider when we approach this passage of Scripture:

1. <u>Women Praying and Prophesying</u> (vv. 3-16) - It seems that some of the women had been swept off their feet by their new found liberty in Christ and they were discarding the established customs of modesty of that day. They refused to cover their

heads when they participated in public services. In that day, except for the temple prostitutes, the women wore long hair and, in public, wore a covering over their heads. For the Christian women in the church, to appear in public without this covering, let alone to pray and share the Word, was both daring and blasphemous.

Paul makes it plain that it was not appropriate for a man to participate in public worship with something on his head (v. 4). On the contrary, it was wrong for a woman to participate with her head uncovered (v. 5). This covering symbolized her submission and purity.

APPLICATION:

The first question I should ask myself is, *"What does the Bible instruct me to do?"* The second question is, *"Does it offend the ones I want to minister to?"* The third question is *"Will I do it anyway?"*

I CORINTHIANS

Scripture Reading: 11:17-34

Weekly Memory Verse: 11:3

Topic: Lord's Supper

THOUGHTS ABOUT THE PASSAGE:

The next item Paul brings to their attention in this chapter is:

2. The Lord's Supper (vv. 17-34) - The Corinthians were to be commended for keeping the ordinances (v. 2), but they deserved sharp criticism for the manner in which they did so. What should have resulted in spiritual blessing was perpetrating a spirit of division. (Of course, the divisions at the dinner were just evidence of selfishness.) Paul warned the people and even urged them to examine themselves (v. 28).

From the very early days of the church it was customary for the believers to eat together before they partook of the Lord's Table (Acts 2:42, 46). They called this meal "the love feast." This meal was part of the worship of the church at Corinth but some serious abuses had crept in.

1. Various cliques had formed in the church and people were always eating with their own crowd rather than developing fellowship with the whole church family.
2. Rich people brought a great deal of food for them-

selves and didn't share it with those who were poor
and needy. This "agape feast" should have been an
opportunity for edification but instead it was turning
into a time of embarrassment.

3. Some were even turning this special meal time into a
drinking party. This certainly was not the best way
to prepare for the Lord's Supper.

Nothing unites believers more than the forgiveness Jesus
provided when He died for our sins. Therefore it should be
no surprise that He instituted a special Supper before He
went to the cross. He knew we would need to be reminded
often of what He did to make us clean. However, it seems
that the Lord's Supper in the Corinthian church was being
characterized by divisions.

APPLICATION:

I should prepare myself for taking communion through
healthy introspection and confession of sin (vv. 27-31).
Awareness of my sin should not keep me away from
communion but should cause me to want to confess my sin
and make things right so that I can participate in it.

I CORINTHIANS

Scripture Reading: 12:1-11

Weekly Memory Verse: 11:3

Topic: Tongues

THOUGHTS ABOUT THE PASSAGE:

Paul continues his discussion of the subject of irregularities in the worship of the Corinthian church. There was a self-indulgent spirit in the area of spiritual gifts that produced selfishness, disunity and apparent chaos in the assembly (12:7,25). Unfortunately, the members were grieving the Holy Spirit by the carnal ways in which they were using spiritual gifts. While Paul is about to deal with the entire subject of spiritual gifts, it is clear from the start that a special emphasis will be on only one of them, tongues. Of the sign gifts (prophesy, healing and tongues), most conservative Bible scholars say these have ceased but others say they have not. Since it is very difficult to prove either way, this continues to be a debate to this day.

Another issue concerning tongues is whether it was always a known language or sometimes an ecstatic speech. We know for sure that it refers to a known language in Acts. A study of the New Testament usage of *glossa* reveals the fact that it always refers to foreign languages and not some gibberish or unknown sounds. Furthermore, this is inconsistent with the purpose for which Christ gave this gift and it always refers to the ability to speak an unlearned living language. This view has been held by Barnes, Henry, Ironside, Lenski, Rice and many others.

Robert Gromacki, in his book on "The Modern Tongues Movement," says, "Speaking in foreign languages which were not learned would certainly constitute a divine miracle; however, speaking in gibberish can easily be done by either a Christian or an unsaved person and has no objective standard by which it can be evaluated. Therefore it is not logical to assume that God would institute a miracle that men could duplicate through human simulations."

Warren Wiersbe, in his book "Be Wise," page 123), says it is important to note that the believer is always in control of himself when the Holy Spirit is at work because Jesus Christ the Lord is in charge (14:32). Any so called "spirit manifestation" that robs a person on self-control is not of God; for "the fruit of the Spirit is.....self-control" (Gal. 5:22-23).

APPLICATION:

I need to evaluate everything I do as to whether it is for God's glory or my glory.

I CORINTHIANS

Scripture Reading: 12: 12-26

Weekly Memory Verse: 11:3

Topic: Diversity

THOUGHTS ABOUT THE PASSAGE:

You may remember a few years ago when Snoopy, the lovable beagle in the Peanuts cartoon, had his left leg broken. Hundreds wrote letters to Snoopy or sent sympathy cards. Snoopy himself philosophized about his plight one day while perched on top of his doghouse and looking at the huge white cast on his leg. "My body blames my foot for not being able to go places. My foot says it was my head's fault, and my head blamed my eyes.... My eyes say my feet are clumsy, and my right foot says not to blame him for what my left foot did...." Snoopy looks out at his audience and confesses, "I don't say anything because I don't want to get involved." (*Source Unknown*)

Paul reminds us that the gifts are given to unite us in our ministry in the one body and for the good of the whole church. The Holy Spirit bestows these gifts "as He wills" and not as we will (v. 11). No Christian should ever complain about his or her gifts. We are many members in one body, ministering to each other.

In the body there is a diversity of gifts. There is a tendency among Christians for some people to magnify the "sensational" gifts. Some believers feel very guilty because they possess gifts that do not put them in the limelight. It is this attitude that Paul is opposed to and is addressing in this passage. Paul illustrates his point by comparing the different parts of the human body to the different parts of the church. Each member needs the other members, and no member can afford to become independent. When a part of the human body becomes independent, you have a serious problem that often leads to sickness and even death. In a healthy human body, the various members cooperate and even help each other when a crisis occurs. Diversity leads to unity when the members care for each other; but diversity leads to disunity when members compete with one another. If one member suffers, it affects every member. If one member is healthy, it helps the others to be strong. In other words, unless gifts are used in a spirit of love, they are of little value.

APPLICATION:

I must never look down on those who seem unimportant, and I should not be jealous of others who have impressive gifts. Instead, I should use the gifts I have been given and encourage others to use theirs.

I CORINTHIANS

Scripture Reading: 12: 27-31

Weekly Memory Verse: 11:3

Topic: Spiritual Gifts

THOUGHTS ABOUT THE PASSAGE:

This story was related by Donald Grey Barnhouse. Several years ago, two students graduated from the Chicago-Kent College of Law. The highest ranking student in the class was a blind man named Overton and, when he received his honor, he insisted that half the credit should go to his friend, Kaspryzak. They had met one another in school when the armless Mr. Kaspryzak had guided the blind Mr. Overton down a flight of stairs. This acquaintance ripened into friendship and a beautiful example of interdependence. The blind man carried the books which the armless man read aloud in their common study, and thus the individual deficiency of each was compensated for by the other. After their graduation, they planned to practice law together. No believer is complete by himself, we are to minister to one another, as a family. (*Source unknown*).

For a third time, Paul stresses the fact that God, not man, assigned the gifts (vv. 18, 24, 28). God gives to each person and each congregation just the gifts it needs when they are needed. No individual believer possesses all the spiritual gifts. Each believer has the gift (or gifts) assigned to him. The stress is on quality and quantity. In verse 28 Paul gives a further listing of the gifts with some additions to those included in verses 4-11. It seems that the list is arranged in order of the most important first and the least important last. In this arrangement apostles, prophets and teachers are the first three listed and tongues are last. These first three gifts may have been greater because of their extensive value to the whole body of Christ.

The gift of tongues, on the other hand, tended to bring pride and self-centeredness to the people involved. This self-centeredness also manifested itself in other areas such as eating sacrificial foods, women in worship, celebration of the Lord's Supper, etc. Love for others was an essential need in the Corinthian church. He commanded that love should prevail among the members (I John 15:12). This was the ingredient which would maintain unity within the diversity.

APPLICATION:

My spiritual gifts are not for my own self-advancement. They were given to me for the purpose of serving God and enhancing the spiritual growth of other believers.

I CORINTHIANS

Scripture Reading: 13:1-13

Weekly Memory Verse: 11:3

Topic: Love

THOUGHTS ABOUT THE PASSAGE

This is one of the most noted and best-loved chapters in the entire Bible. At the same time, few chapters have suffered more misinterpretation and misapplication than I Corinthians 13. Divorced from its context, it often becomes a sentimental sermon on Christian brotherhood. It is easy to forget that Paul is still dealing with the Corinthian problems of tongues, divisions, envy, selfishness, lawsuits, impatience, etc.

The main evidence of maturity in the Christian life is a growing love for God and for God's people, as well as a love for lost souls. Paul now proceeds to show us the qualities of love:

1. It is not easily roused to resentment (v. 4).
2. It has the idea of being useful (v. 4).
3. It does not sound its own praises (v. 4).
4. It is not swelled with pride (v. 4).
5. It is not easily provoked (v. 5).
6. It does not keep track of the offenses committed against it (v. 5).
7. It does not take delight in that which is offensive to

God (v. 6).

8. It rejoices when truth is proclaimed (v. 6).
9. It covers all things (v. 7).
10. It will believe well of others unless convinced otherwise (v. 7).
11. It is always positive and hopeful (v. 7).
12. It sustains the assaults of an enemy (v. 7).

Unlike many of the spiritual gifts, love will never be outmoded, unnecessary or eliminated. As a child my speech was undeveloped, my understanding and knowledge incomplete. But when I became a man my speech became subject to His mind, His understanding, and His knowledge, which is complete.

APPLICATION:

The more I become like Christ, the more love I will show to others.

I CORINTHIANS

Scripture Reading: 14:1-9

Weekly Memory Verse: 11:3

Topic: Tongues

THOUGHTS ABOUT THE PASSAGE:

From the various gifts mentioned in chapter 12, the apostle selects three for discussion in this chapter. These are (1) prophecy, (2) speaking in tongues, (3) and interpretation of tongues. Paul compares and contrasts the Corinthians' preoccupation with tongues and their apparent disinterest in prophecy. They apparently were quite proud of the fact that they could speak in tongues and were using it as a sign of spiritual superiority. Paul shows that this gift is much less important than others, and that it is not to be used in public at all, unless certain requirements are met. Spiritual gifts are beneficial only when they are used to help everyone in the church. We should not exercise them to make ourselves feel good. "He that speaketh in an unknown tongue edifieth himself; but he that prophesieth edifieth the church" (v. 14).

It is well to remember that Paul regarded tongues as the least to be desired of all the gifts of the spirit, and found it necessary to warn the Corinthian Christians against the abuse and improper estimate of this gift. It is unfortunate that our translators have inserted the word "unknown" into the text. The word "unknown" is in italics, meaning that it is not to be found in the original Greek text of the New

Testament. So Paul refers here to one who is able to "speak in a tongue." Other references to this gift are to be found only in Mark 16:17, Acts 2, Acts 10, and Acts 19. On the day of Pentecost the disciples spoke not in "unknown" tongues, but in actual languages.

Paul used the word "glossa" 21 times in I Corinthians, and three times in his other letters. Wolvoord and Zuck in their "Bible Knowledge Commentary" have this to say about the meaning of the word: "Whether it was used literally of the physical organ or figuratively of human language, it nowhere referred to as ecstatic speech. If it is unreasonable to interpret the unknown with the help of the known, the obscure by the clear, then the burden of proof rests with those who find in this term a meaning other than human language." Warren Wiersbe says, "From the very beginning of the church, tongues were known languages, recognized by listeners. The tongue would be unknown to the speaker and to the listener, but it was not unknown in the world."

APPLICATION:

I should never exercise any spiritual gift just to make myself feel good.

I CORINTHIANS

Scripture Reading: 14:10-17

Weekly Memory Verse: 14:22

Topic: Communication

THOUGHTS ABOUT THE PASSAGE:

The story is told about three kids bragging about their fathers: The first one said, "My dad's so smart he can talk for one hour on any subject." The second one said, "My dad's so smart he can talk for two hours on any subject." Finally, the third one said, "My dad's so smart he can talk for 3 hours and doesn't even need a subject." (*Source unknown*).

Paul's statement in verse 10 gives us good reason to believe that he was referring to known languages and not some "heavenly" language. Each known language is different and yet it has its own meaning. No matter how sincere a speaker may be, if I do not understand his language, he cannot communicate with me. No one can be understood unless their messages are communicated in a manner that is meaningful to the listener.

In verses 12-15 Paul reminds the Corinthians that it is better to be a blessing to the church than to experience some kind of personal "spiritual excitement." If a person is able to speak in a tongue (language) he is not familiar with, his spirit (inner person) may share in the experience, but his mind is not a part of the experience. The word "spirit" in verses 14-15 does not refer to the Holy Spirit, but to the inner person. If the speaker is to be edified personally, he must understand what he is saying and this requires an interpreter. This means that an interpreter needs to be present or the speaker himself has the gift of interpreting.

There is a proper place for the intellect in Christianity. In praying and singing, both the mind and the spirit are to be fully engaged (v. 15). When we sing, we should think about the meaning of the words we are singing. When we pour out our feelings to God in prayer, we should not turn off our capacity to think. True Christianity is neither barren intellectualism nor thoughtless emotionalism. All of this discussion emphasized once again the superiority of prophecy over tongues: prophecy needs no interpretation and can therefore be a blessing to everybody.

APPLICATION:

This is a reminder to me that when I speak, I need to say things in such a way that they can easily be understood, whether to my wife, my children or to those that I come in contact with.

I CORINTHIANS

Scripture Reading: 14: 18-25

Weekly Memory Verse: 14:22

Topic: Understanding

THOUGHTS ABOUT THE PASSAGE:

As a nation, the Jews were always seeking a sign (Matt. 12:38, I Cor. 1:22). At Pentecost, the fact that the apostles spoke in tongues was a sign to the unbelieving Jews who were there celebrating the feast. The miracle of tongues aroused their interest, but it did not convict their hearts. It took Peter's preaching (in Aramaic, which all the people understood) to bring them to the place of conviction and conversion. Have you ever heard a preacher who was trying to impress his audience with how much Greek he knew by quoting a lot of it to the audience? It may have made him feel good as to all that he was able to quote but it really didn't do a thing for the people listening.

In this passage Paul makes it plain that it is not quantity of words but the quality of communication that is important. He says that in their tongues speaking, the church members in Corinth are acting like children playing with toys and not as mature men (v. 20). Paul associates the gift of tongues with spiritual immaturity. He implies that as the church matures, their concerns will be less in the area of the spectacular and more in the area of understanding. The purpose of tongues was to demonstrate God's divine power to the unbeliever (v. 22). It took preaching in the language that people understood to bring them to the place of conviction and conversion. A message in a language that the people could not understand (unless interpreted) could never bring conviction to the heart of a lost sinner. In fact, the unsaved person might leave the service thinking the whole assembly was crazy (v. 23).

Paul taught in Koine Greek as well as in Aramaic, which all the Jews spoke. He also spoke in ancient Hebrew and all of his New Testament epistles were written in Greek. Therefore, he could rightly say that he spoke more in foreign languages than any of his audience (v. 18). Nevertheless, he insisted that he would rather speak five words that could be understood than ten thousand words in a language with which his hearers were unfamiliar (v. 19).

APPLICATION:

This should be a vivid reminder to me that when I share the Word of God, it must be understood if it is to do anyone any good. That is why the appropriate use of illustrations provides a window of understanding to truth in the Word that is unfamiliar to the listener.

I CORINTHIANS

Scripture Reading: 14:26-40

Weekly Memory Verse: 14:22

Topic: Organization

THOUGHTS ABOUT THE PASSAGE:

In a Peanuts cartoon Lucy demanded that Linus change TV channels, threatening him with her fist if he didn't. "What makes you think you can walk right in here and take over?" asks Linus. "These five fingers," says Lucy. "Individually they're nothing but when I curl them together like this into a single fist, they form a weapon that is mighty to behold." "Which channel do you want?" asks Linus. Turning away, he looks at his fingers and says, "Why can't you guys get organized like that?" (*Peanuts Cartoon*).

Two things are specifically emphasized in this passage:

1. "Let all things be done unto edifying" (v. 26).
2. "Let all things be done decently and in order" (v. 40).

This has been the theme in this chapter and continues in Paul's thinking as he gives instruction for worship in the church. Worship services in the early church do not seem to have been dominated by one individual, but open to free participation by all who would choose to participate. It is evident that the Corinthian church was having special problems with disorders in their public meetings. Furthermore, it seems that the tongues speakers were the ones causing the most trouble, so Paul addressed himself to them and gave specific instructions for the church to follow in their services.

1. There must never be more than three speaking in tongues in any one meeting (v. 27).
2. To speak in tongues without an interpreter is forbidden (v. 28).
3. Women are not permitted to speak in tongues in the church services (v.34).

Certainly, Paul was not saying that women had no right to pray or share God's Word in the church, because he had already given instructions as to how she was to do this (11:5).

APPLICATION:

Lord, help me to be on the lookout as to how I can edify other Christians and to always be organized to the point that others will feel comfortable in the things I do.

I CORINTHIANS

Scripture Reading: 15:1-11

Weekly Memory Verse: 14:22

Topic: Resurrection

THOUGHTS ABOUT THE PASSAGE:

As Vice President, George Bush represented the U.S. at the funeral of former Soviet leader Leonid Brezhnev, he was deeply moved by a silent protest carried out by Brezhnev's widow. She stood motionless by the coffin until seconds before it was closed. Then, just as the soldiers touched the lid, Brezhnev's wife performed an act of great courage and hope. She reached down and made the sign of the cross on her husband's chest. There in the center of secular, atheistic power, the wife of the man who had run it all hoped that her husband was wrong. She hoped that there was another life, and that life was best represented by Jesus who died on the cross, and that the same Jesus might yet have mercy on her husband. (*Gary Thomas, in Christianity Today, October 3, 1994*).

Paul has finished his answers to the Corinthians' questions, and he now goes on to a new subject. It has been said that this is truly the great resurrection chapter of the entire Bible. The first eleven verses present the Gospel message and the evidence for its truthfulness. Paul gives three proofs to his readers that Jesus Christ has indeed been raised from the dead:

1. Their salvation (vv. 1,2): Paul had preached the Gospel (which included Christ's resurrection) and their faith had transformed their lives. After all, a dead savior cannot save anybody.
2. The Old Testament Scriptures (vv. 3,4): The Old Testament declared Jesus' resurrection on the third day in the experience of Jonah. Other proof texts are Acts 2:25-28; 13:32-33.
3. The fact that He was seen by many witnesses (vv. 5-11): Peter saw Him, the disciples saw Him collectively (v. 5). Five hundred plus people saw Him at the same time (v. 6) and James, Jesus' half-brother saw Him (v. 7). The greatest witness of the resurrection was Paul himself.

In humility Paul did not magnify his own personal credentials, but only the sovereign grace of God as he states; "But by the grace of God I am what I am." Lord, help this to be my testimony also.

APPLICATION:

True humility is not convincing myself that I am worthless, but recognizing God's work in me. Paul shares how God wants to accomplish many things through my life, but only because of His mercy and not because we deserve anything.

I CORINTHIANS

Scripture Reading: 15:12-19

Weekly Memory Verse: 14:22

Topic: Resurrection

THOUGHTS ABOUT THE PASSAGE:

D. L. Moody, the great evangelist of the nineteenth century, assigned some ministerial students to conduct evangelistic tent meetings throughout the city of Chicago. The students were to preach nightly sermons as a means of winning souls for Christ and to practice their preaching. Dr. Moody personally showed up one night unannounced at one of the meeting places to hear one of his fledgling young ministers preach the gospel. The young man did quite well expounding on the death of Christ on the cross for the sins of the world. At the close of the service, he announced that everyone should come back the next night when he would "preach on the resurrection of Christ." After the people left, Moody said, "Young man, many of these people will not be back tomorrow night and consequently have only heard half the gospel!" (*Source unknown*).

Most Greeks did not believe that a person's body would be resurrected after death. They thought the soul would enter some eternal state but not the body. Christianity, by contrast, affirms that the body and soul will be reunited after the resurrection. These verses reveal the essential nature of the resurrection of Christ so far as Christian truth is concerned.

There were people in Corinth who were saying there was no resurrection. Paul presents logical consequences of denying the resurrection:

12. If there is no resurrection, then Jesus Christ is still in the grave (v. 16).
13. If He is not raised, there is no gospel to preach (v. 17).
14. If there is no gospel, then you have believed in vain and you are still in your sins (v. 17).
15. If there is no resurrection, then believers who have died have no hope (v. 18).

Faith in a dead Savior means that our religious beliefs are of no value. If our hope in Christ does not take us beyond this life, then "we are of all men most miserable" (v. 19). Because we know that Christ did rise from the dead, we have the certainty that our sins have been forgiven and that He now lives in the presence of the Father and represents us to Him.

APPLICATION:

If I do not believe in the resurrection of Jesus Christ as the Bible teaches, my belief about everything else is meaningless. I serve a living and not a dead Christ.

I CORINTHIANS

Scripture Reading: 15:20-28

Weekly Memory Verse: 14:22

Topic: Resurrection

THOUGHTS ABOUT THE PASSAGE:

In the first half of this chapter Paul dealt with *the resurrection of Christ*. Now, in the last half of the chapter he deals with *the resurrection of Christians*. Christ arose and so shall we who know Him. Paul had explored the logical happenings which followed the denial of the bodily resurrection of Christ (vv. 12-19). He now explores the theological argument that the destiny of Christians was bound up in the destiny of Christ, and he set forth the positive consequences of this union. The big question is - When are the dead raised? Paul used three images to answer that question.

1. Firstfruits (vv. 20,23) - The term "first fruits" refers to the Lord Jesus Himself (v. 20). When the priest in Israel waved the sheaf of the first fruits before the Lord, it was a sign that the entire harvest belonged to Him. When Jesus was raised from the dead, it was God's sign (assurance) to us that we shall also be raised one day (at the rapture) to be with Him (v. 21).
2. Adam (vv. 21-22) - Paul saw in Adam a type of Jesus Christ by the way of contrast. The first Adam disobeyed God and brought sin and death into the world (Rom 5:12-21), but the last Adam (Jesus

Christ) obeyed the Father and brought life and hope (v. 22).

3. <u>The Kingdom</u> (vv. 24-28) - When Jesus comes to this earth to judge, He will banish sin for a thousand years (referred to as "the millennium") and establish His kingdom (Rev. 20:1-6). But after this period of time there will be one final rebellion against God which Jesus will end with one final judgment (Rev. 20:7-10). The lost will be raised, judged, and cast into the lake of fire for ever and ever.

It is evident that God has an order or a sequence of events that He follows in the resurrection. There is certainly no such thing as a "general resurrection" taught in the Scriptures. Revelation 20 makes it clear that the dead are raised in two groups, with the millennium coming between. The Lord Jesus will have finally and completely put down all hostile powers and authority. Even death itself will at last be destroyed.

APPLICATION:

World events may seem out of control and justice may seem scarce, but I can be sure that God is in control and things will come to pass according to His time table.

I CORINTHIANS

Scripture Reading: 15:29-34

Weekly Memory Verse: 14:22

Topic: Relationships

THOUGHTS ABOUT THE PASSAGE:

What does it mean in verse 29 when it says to be "baptized for the dead"? The Bible Knowledge Commentary says that "up to 200 explanations have been given for this verse. Some, such as the Mormons, believe it means "proxy baptism", where a believer is baptized on behalf of a dead relative; but there is no reference to this in the entire New Testament. In fact, scripture makes it plain that baptism never saves anyone. Possibly some in Corinth were propounding this false view of baptism and Paul simply used it as an argument against those who denied the resurrection. Paul's concluding advice with reference to those who continued to deny the resurrection was not to associate with them. Previously he had compared immorality in the church to yeast in bread (5:6-7).

The phrase, "I die daily" (v. 31), refers to the physical dangers Paul faced as a servant of Christ (II Cor. 11:23-28). Paul's life was in such constant jeopardy that he never knew when he might be called upon to give his life. He makes it plain that sacrifice in Christian service such as he was making would be useless if there was no resurrection. Furthermore, if there is no resurrection, then what we do with our bodies will have no bearing on our future. Immorality was a way of life in Corinth, and some of the believers rejected the resurrection in order to rationalize their sin.

Paul goes on to tell the Christians that they need to wake up to righteousness and quit thinking that they are spiritually superior. The denial of the resurrection suggests that those who hold to such a view are literally "ignorant of God." It was shameful that the church in Corinth had allowed people in their assembly to have called such an important truth into question. Bad company corrupts good character. False teachers should be avoided (II Cor. 6:14-7:1). So Paul insists that the Corinthians must not associate with those who say that there is no resurrection, for this would be to risk an infection which can pollute life. To say that there is no resurrection is not a sign of superior knowledge; it is a sign of utter ignorance of God.

APPLICATION:

I must never let my relationships with unbelievers lead me away from Christ or cause my faith to waiver. It is very important whom I choose as my close friends.

I CORINTHIANS

Scripture Reading: 15:35-44

Weekly Memory Verse: 14:22

Topic: Body

THOUGHTS ABOUT THE PASSAGE:

In March of 1981, President Reagan was shot by John Hinckley, Jr. , and was hospitalized for several weeks. Although Reagan was the nation's chief executive, his hospitalization had little impact on the nation's activity. Government continued. On the other hand, suppose the garbage collectors in this country went on strike, as they did in Philadelphia not long ago. That city was not only in a literal mess, but the pile of decaying trash quickly became a health hazard. A three-week nationwide strike would paralyze the country. Who is more important—the President or a garbage collector? In the body of Christ, seemingly insignificant ones are urgently needed. As Paul reminds us, "The head cannot say to the feet, 'I don't need you!' On the contrary, those parts of the body that seem to be weaker are indispensable (I Cor. 12:21–22)." - David Parsons (*Source unknown*).

The apostle Paul opens up discussion concerning the nature of the resurrection body. He deals with two questions which foolish objectors raise (v. 35). The first question implies that resurrection is impossible; the second, that it is inconceivable.

1. "How are the dead raised up?"

2. "With what body do they come?"

A comparison is made between the resurrection of our bodies and the growth of a plant in the field. Seeds planted in the ground don't grow unless they "die" first (v. 36). The plant that grows looks very different from the seed because God gives it a new body (v. 38). Our resurrection body will be somewhat, but not altogether different from our earthly body. The resurrection body is related to the earthly body in the same sense that the plant is related to the seed. This should not seem strange because there are different kinds of bodies here on earth in the animal kingdom (v. 39). There are also differences in bodies adapted to the heavenly realm and those adapted to the earthly realm (v. 40). Our present bodies are perishable and prone to decay. They are temporal, and weak.

APPLICATION:

If the body I am living in on this earth gives me trouble, I can claim the victory because I am going to have a body in heaven that is perfect. What a day that will be!

I CORINTHIANS

Scripture Reading: 15:45-50

Weekly Memory Verse: 15:58

Topic: Changed

THOUGHTS ABOUT THE PASSAGE:

It was not until 1850 that our world reached the one billion mark. By 1930 we reached two billion. It took only thirty more years for the world's population to reach three billion. We have now arrived at six billion. Statisticians tell us that by the end of this century we'll have over seven billion. Until 1800 the top speed was twenty miles an hour as people traveled on horseback. With the arrival of the railroad train, almost overnight we jumped to 100 miles per hour. By 1952 the first passenger jet could travel 500 miles an hour. By 1979 the Concorde cruised at more than 1,200 miles an hour. But even back in 1961 the astronauts were orbiting the earth at 16,000 miles per hour. (*C. Swindoll, Rise and Shine, 1989*).

In our passage today we are told about a bigger change than this. In the previous passage, we were told that the body is buried in corruption because it is going to decay; but it is raised with such a nature that it cannot decay. With this change there is no decay or death in heaven. The expression "last Adam," in verse 45, was coined by the Apostle Paul as a reference to Christ. Today we have a "natural body," that is, a body suited to an earthly environment. We received this body from our first parent, Adam. Adam was made from the dust of the ground and so are we (Gen. 2:7). Our resurrection body will be made in the image of Jesus Christ, the last Adam. In His resurrection body, He was able to move quickly from place to place, even through locked doors; yet He was able to eat food and His disciples were able to touch and feel Him (John 20:19-29).

The point that Paul seems to be making in this passage is that the resurrection body completes the work of redemption and transforms us into the image of our Savior. We are made in the image of God, as far as personality is concerned. We are made in the image of Adam, as far as the body is concerned. One day we will bear the image of our Savior, when we are in heaven. Our first birth gave us that which is natural, but our second birth gives us that which is spiritual. God rejects the first birth and says, "Ye must be born again!" If we depend on our first birth, we will be condemned forever; but if we experience the new birth, we shall live with Christ forever.

APPLICATION:

When I am resurrected, God will give me a changed, eternal body suited to my new eternal life.

I CORINTHIANS

Scripture Reading: 15:51-58

Weekly Memory Verse: 15:58

Topic: Steadfast

THOUGHTS ABOUT THE PASSAGE:

William Carey, the "father of modern missions," wanted to translate the Bible into as many Indian languages as possible. He established a large print-shop in Serampore where translation work was continually being done. Carey spent hours each day translating Scripture, often while his insane wife ranted and raved in the next room. Then one night his print shop, where the Bibles were being printed, burned to the ground. Yet Carey persevered , and went forward and accomplished his goal. The secret of Carey's success is found in his steadfast determination. He once wrote: "There are grave difficulties on every hand, and more are looming ahead. Therefore we must go forward." (*Source Unknown*).

Paul's doctrinal declarations led to practical directives and this chapter's conclusion was no exception. We will be given new bodies when Christ returns and these bodies will be without disabilities (vv. 52-53). This means that death should no longer be a source of fear for the Christian, but a time of anticipation. Death has been defeated and we have hope beyond the grave (vv. 54-56).

In verse 58, Paul says that because of the Resurrection,

nothing we do is in vain. No man can take credit for this victory. It comes through our Lord Jesus Christ (v. 57). Because of it, we should be *"steadfast, unmovable, always abounding in the work of the Lord."* We can be sure that one day we will share in the glory of His resurrection.

1. To be steadfast means to be consistent. You do not have to be flashy, but the Lord expects faithful obedience to the tasks and relationships He has called us to minister through.
2. To be unmoveable. Often we think that we cannot bend or we will break. Unmoveable does not necessarily mean legalistic, brittle or unbending, but to be unshakable, and unbreakable.
3. To be abounding is to give yourself fully to the work of the Lord. We are not to grow weary in well doing, but to be stretchable and extremely flexible.

APPLICATION:

Sometimes I hesitate to do good because I don't see any immediate results. I just need to keep in mind that nothing I do is in vain (v. 58). Victory is mine through Jesus Christ, my Lord.

I CORINTHIANS

Scripture Reading: 16:1-12

Weekly Memory Verse: 15:58

Topic: Giving

THOUGHTS ABOUT THE PASSAGE:

On the way home from church the father was complaining, "That church service, the sermon was too long, the music was too loud and the building was too hot." His son in the back seat replied, "I don't know, Dad, I thought it was a pretty good show for a buck." (*Source unknown*).

In this passage, Paul answers a question the Corinthian believers had asked about a collection he was taking for the poor and then shares his personal travel plans. The Corinthians had apparently heard from the Galatian churches that he was taking an offering for the poor in Jerusalem. How we handle our finances is often a good measure of our relationship with the Lord. In answering their question about money, Paul gives some important principles on giving (vv. 1-4):

1. <u>Offerings need to be made regularly</u>, "Upon the first day of the week" (vv. 1-2).
2. <u>Every person needs to give</u>, whether rich or poor (v. 2). Jesus commanded in Mt. 10:8, "Freely you have received, freely give."
3. <u>Giving is to be proportionate</u>, not just a little (v. 2).

4. The money needs to be handled honestly (vv. 3-4). It is unfortunate that many Christian ministries lose their testimony because they mismanage funds.

Paul was as careful in his use of time as he was in his use of money. Someone has said that killing time is the chief occupation of modern society. The apostle shares his travel plans so he can take advantage of every opportunity (vv. 5-9). He was in Ephesus when he wrote this letter. From there he planned to travel to Macedonia for a time of ministry, being in Corinth during the winter, when it would be difficult to travel. Then he was to go to Judea to make the collection. However, because of various circumstances, his plans had to be revised at least twice and he ended up not spending as much time in Corinth as he had hoped or as they had expected.

APPLICATION:

I need to ask God each day what opportunities He is giving to me. Instead of complaining about the obstacles I have, I need to take advantage of the opportunities and leave the results with the Lord.

I CORINTHIANS

Scripture Reading: 16:13-16

Weekly Memory Verse: 15:58

Topic: Commitment

THOUGHTS ABOUT THE PASSAGE:

Paul begins a series of closing remarks, exhortations, challenges, and greetings. Faith, conviction, courage, and love are essential ingredients for success and victory. As the Corinthians wait for Paul's next visit, he exhorts them to a fivefold commitment:

4. "Watch ye" - (Be alert! Be on your guard!) - (v. 13).
5. "Stand fast in the faith" - (Have mature stability) - (v. 13).
6. "Quit you like men" - (Act like men, not children) - (v. 13).
7. "Be strong" - (not physically, but spiritually) - (v. 13).
8. "Let all things be done with charity" - (love) - (v. 14).

Stephanas and his family were the first people to be won to Christ in Achaia. Achaia was the Roman province extending over central and southern Greece, of which Corinth was the capital. They became important leaders in the church, for they committed themselves to the service of Christ. It seems that whenever they saw a need, they went to work to meet it without having to be asked. They were Paul's helpers and labored with him faithfully in the church. Paul recognized them as ordained by God and he encouraged the others to submit to their leadership. *One primary qualification for leadership in the church today is a willingness to serve.* Many people today want to be served rather than being willing to serve.

The **holy kiss** (cf. 2 Cor. 13:12; Rom. 16:16; 1 Thes. 5:25; 1 Peter 5:14) was primarily an expression of the love, forgiveness, and unity which should exist among Christians. This kiss of peace was a lovely custom of the early Church. It may have been a Jewish custom which the early Church took over. It was apparently given at the end of the prayers and just before the congregation partook of the sacrament. It was the sign and symbol that they sat at the table of love joined in perfect love.

APPLICATION:

Carl Sandberg, when addressing the United States Congress, said that Abraham Lincoln was a man of "velvet steel." As a Christian, I need to remember that true manliness does not do away with tenderness.

I CORINTHIANS

Scripture Reading: 16:17-24

Weekly Memory Verse: 15:58

Topic: Commendation

THOUGHTS ABOUT THE PASSAGE:

As Paul comes to the close of his letter, he talks about some of his friends who have helped him in the ministry. Stephanas, Fortunatus and Achaicus were part of a committee sent from Corinth to Ephesus to confer with Paul about church problems. However, these men did more than share problems; they also refreshed his spirit and brought him blessing. It is so easy for us to share only problems and burdens with our spiritual leaders and rarely share the blessings.

He also tells us about Aquila and Priscilla, a husband-and-wife team, who had been expelled from Rome because Aquila was a Jew. They had come to Corinth and set up a tent-making business and this was where Paul first met them. When Paul moved from Corinth to Ephesus, they packed up their business and moved with him to assist in founding the church in that city. They were such a capable couple, that he left them to oversee the ministry when he returned to Antioch.

An interesting sidelight is that in those early days there were no church buildings. It was not until the third century that we hear about a church building at all. The little congregations met in private houses. If a house had a room big enough, it was there that the Christian fellowship met. Now wherever Aquila and Priscilla went, their home became a church. When they are in Rome, Paul sends greetings to them and to the church that is their house (Romans 16:3–5). When he writes from Ephesus, he sends greetings from them and from the church that is in their house. Aquila and Priscilla made their home a center of Christian light and love, and a haven of rest, peace and friendship for the lonely, the tempted, the sad, and the depressed.

Later, when Paul writes to the saints in Rome, he greets them (Rom. 16:3). Then in I Timothy 4:19, this remarkable couple had left Rome and were now back in Ephesus to assist Timothy. How many couples today would move as often as Aquila and Priscilla, just to be able to serve the Lord better?

APPLICATION:

I would like to be known for the hospitality that Aquila and Priscilla were known for. Lord, help me to be a person who is looking for ways to help and encourage other people.

MEMORY VERSES
(I Corinthians)

- <u>Memorize One Verse Each Week As A Family</u> -

Week #1

"For the preaching of the cross is to them that perish foolishness; but unto us which are saved it is the power of God." *I Cor. 1:18*

Week #2

"Moreover it is required in stewards, that a man be found faithful." *I Cor. 4:2*

Week #3

"What? Know ye not that your body is the temple of the Holy Ghost which is in you, which ye have of God, and ye are not your own? For ye are bought with a price: therefore glorify God in your body, and in your spirit, which are God's." *I Cor. 6:19-20*

Week #4

"There hath no temptation taken you but such as is common to man: but God *is* faithful, who will not suffer you to be tempted above that ye are able; but will with the temptation also make a way to escape, that ye may be able to bear *it*." *I Cor. 10:13*

Week #5

"But I would have you know, that the head of every man is Christ; and the head of the woman is the man; and the head of Christ is God." *I Cor. 11:3*

Week #6

"Wherefore tongues are for a sign, not to them that believe, but to them that believe not: but prophesying serveth not for them that believe not, but for them which believe." *I Cor. 14:22*

Week #7

"Therefore, my beloved brethren, be ye steadfast, unmoveable, always abounding in the work of the Lord, forasmuch as ye know that your labor is not in vain in the Lord." *I Cor. 15:58*

RESOURCES

1. Vines Expository Dictionary of New Testament Words by W.E. Vine, M.A. (Fleming H. Revell Co., Old Tappan, New Jersey: 1940).

2. The Bible Knowledge Commentary by Wolvoord and Zuck. (Victor Books, Wheaton, IL: 1986).

3. Liberty Bible Commentary Volume II by Hindson and Kroll (The Old Time Gospel Hour, Lynchburg, VA: 1982).

4. The Bible Exposition Commentary Volume I by Warren W. Wiersbe. (Chariot Victor Publishing, Colorado Springs, CO: 1989).

5. The Letters to the Corinthians by William Barclay. (The Westminister Press, Philadelphia, PA: 1975).

6. First Corinthians by G. Coleman Luck. (Moody Press, Chicago, IL: 1958).

7. Be Wise by Warren Wiersbe. (Victor Books, Wheaton, IL: 1983).

2nd

Corinthians

Critics Answered

Part of A Devotional Commentary Series

By Lou Nicholes

PASSAGE AND TOPIC INDEX

INTRODUCTION TO
II CORINTHIANS
Critics Answered

- Paul probably wrote his first letter to the Corinthians in the spring of the year and his second one before winter the same year.

- Second Corinthians 1:1 indicates that this letter was to be shared with other believers in the Roman province of Achaia.

- Corinth had a reputation for prosperity, but she was also a byword for evil living. It was the place where the Isthmiasn Games were held, which were second only to the Olympics.

- This book is an outpouring of the Apostle Paul's heart towards a group of believers in a church which he had founded and which he dearly loved.

- On Paul's second missionary journey he had visited Corinth, a city in the southwest corner of Greece, where he preached the gospel and spent 18 months establishing the church.

- Later Paul had written a letter (I Corinthians) to them in which he dealt with grave and pressing problems confronting the church.

- We cannot be sure as to all that took place between I and II Corinthians but it seems that Paul made a visit to Corinth and found that the problems that occasioned the first letter had not been solved (13:1-2). Following this visit he wrote to the church, a severe and sorrowful letter which in all probability was lost in its entirety (2:4).

- After receiving the good news from Titus that the church had repented Paul writes this letter from Philippi (in Macedonia), hoping to visit them again soon (12:14).

- Keep in mind that these Corinthian believers were subjected to persecution from enemies without and to treachery from enemies within their group.

- Few passages in the Bible so clearly present the case for sacrificial giving as Chapter 8:1-9:15.

- As we read this intensely personal letter we need to listen to Paul's words of love and exhortation. We see his commitment to the truth of the Word of God.

- A suggested Outline:

  1. Paul and his Commission. (Chapters 1-5)
  2. Paul and his Converts. (Chapters 6-9)
  3. Paul and his Critics. (Chapters 10-13)

II CORINTHIANS

Scripture Reading: 1:1-11

Weekly Memory Verse: 3:5

Topic: Comfort

THOUGHTS ABOUT THE PASSAGE:

One night while conducting an evangelistic meeting in the Salvation Army Citadel in Chicago, Booth Tucker preached on the sympathy of Jesus. After his message a man approached him and said, "If your wife had just died, like mine has, and your babies were crying for their mother, who would never come back, you wouldn't be saying what you're saying." Tragically, a few days later, Tucker's wife was killed in a train wreck. Her body was brought to Chicago and carried to the same Citadel for the funeral. After the service the bereaved preacher looked down into the silent face of his wife and then turned to those attending. "The other day a man told me I wouldn't speak of the sympathy of Jesus if my wife had just died. If that man is here, I want to tell him that Christ is sufficient. My heart is broken, but it has a song put there by Jesus. I want that man to know that Jesus Christ speaks comfort to me today." (*Today in the Word, MBI, October, 1991, p. 10*).

Have you ever wondered, why do the righteous suffer? In various portions of Scripture we find that suffering is the result of Adam's original sin which plunged the human race into misery. However, in this portion of Scripture Paul teaches us why it is necessary for the Christian to pass through fiery trials. There are some sufferings that we endure simply because we are human and subject to pain; but there are other sufferings that come because we are God's children and are serving Him. The Corinthians were exposed to testings, not because they were especially wicked, but because tribulation is the portion of all believers.

We must never think that trouble is an accident because for the believer, everything is a divine appointment. God has to work in us before He can work through us. In times of suffering, most of us are prone to think only of ourselves and to forget others. However, suffering can help us minister to others. In every church, there are mature saints of God who have suffered and because of it they are great encouragers. Paul experienced trouble, not as punishment for something he had done but as preparation for something he was yet going to do in ministering to others in need.

APPLICATION:

When have I, because of God's comfort in a previous struggle, been able to comfort someone else in a similar situation? I need to look for opportunities!

II CORINTHIANS

Scripture Reading: 1:12-14

Weekly Memory Verse: 3:5

Topic: Boasting

THOUGHTS ABOUT THE PASSAGE:

In this text it appears that there were those who were attributing hidden motives to Paul. His answer is that his whole conduct is dominated, not by shrewdness, but by the grace of God. *There were no hidden motives in Paul's life.* If we are honest, we will have to admit that we seldom do anything with absolutely unmixed motives. Even when we do something good, there may be entangled with it motives of wanting recognition, of prestige, of something in return. Men may never see these motives, but, as Thomas Aquinas said, "Man regardeth the deed but God seeth the intention." Purity of action may be difficult, but purity of motive is still more difficult. Such purity can come to us only when we too can say that our old self has died and Christ lives in us.

The people of Paul's day must have been saying that there was more in Paul's conduct than met the eye. His answer is that he has lived with the holiness and the purity of God. *There were no hidden actions in his life.* We might well add a new beatitude to the list, "Blessed is the man who has nothing to hide. The word *purity,* that Paul uses, is most interesting (v. 12). It may describe something which can bear the test of being held up to the light of the sun and looked at with the sun shining through it. Happy is the man whose every action will bear the light of day and who, like Paul, can claim that there are no hidden actions in his life.

While it is true that a crisis helps to make a person, it is also true that a crises helps to reveal what a person is made of. It is not love for the lost nor love for the world which distinguishes the believer but love for one another (John 13:35). These believers were Paul's spiritual children. Many of them knew him in a very personal way. In the days when he founded their church and grounded them in the Word of God, they could sense his true heart beat. Paul's letters were like his conduct: simple and sincere; not written from human wisdom but from God's grace (v. 12). He was guided by a love for others and sought what was in their best interests.

APPLICATION:

In Paul's life there were no hidden actions, no hidden motives and no hidden meanings. That is indeed ;a quality of life that I should be striving for.

II CORINTHIANS

Scripture Reading: 1:15-22

Weekly Memory Verse: 3:5

Topic: Promises

THOUGHTS ABOUT THE PASSAGE:

C.S. Lewis in his biography tells of the suffering he endured because he kept a promise he had made to a buddy during World War I. This friend was worried about the care of his wife and small daughter if he should be killed in battle, so Lewis assured him that if that were to happen he would look after them. As the war dragged on, the man was killed. True to his word, Lewis took care of his friend's family. Yet no matter how helpful he tried to be, the woman was ungrateful, rude, arrogant, and domineering. Through it all, Lewis kept forgiving her. He refused to let her actions become an excuse to renege on his promise. (*Source Unknown*).

Misunderstandings are often very difficult to untangle, because one misunderstanding often leads to another. This is what had happened to Paul as he was forced to make a change of plans. In Paul's initial itinerary, he had intended to go immediately from Ephesus to Corinth and spend the winter. When that didn't work out he had planned to travel to Macedonia and then back to Corinth if the Lord permitted him to do so (I Cor. 16:2-8). Much to Paul's regret and embarrassment, he had to cancel both plan A and plan B. When we consider how difficult both transportation and communication were in that day, it is a miracle that Paul did not have more problems with his busy schedule.

With this change in plans, Paul's opponents accused him of following fleshly wisdom (v. 12), of being careless with the will of God (v. 17), and making plans just to please himself. These false apostles hoped to discredit their chief rival (11:4,13). Paul had informed the church about his change in plans, but this did not silence the opposition. They were saying,"If Paul says or writes one thing, he really means another! His yes is no, and his no is yes" (vv. 17-18). No matter what his accusers said, Paul stood firm because he had a clear conscience. He knew that his motives were sincere; he was seeking to please the Lord and not men.

APPLICATION:

Have you ever been forced to change your plans, which others did not understand, and they made a big issue about it? When I am forced to make a choice between doing what I know the Lord wants me to do and what others are saying, I must always follow the Lord.

II CORINTHIANS

Scripture Reading: 1:23-2:4

Weekly Memory Verse: 3:5

Topic: Leadership

THOUGHTS ABOUT THE PASSAGE:

When John Knox was on his deathbed he said, "God knows that my mind was always void of hatred to the persons of those against whom I thundered my severest judgments." It is possible to hate the sin but love the sinner. Effective rebuke is the kind that is given with the arm of love around the other person. Rebuke given in the spirit of anger may hurt and even terrify; but the rebuke given in a loving spirit can break the heart. When Paul rebuked, the last thing he wanted was to be domineering. Effective leadership is sensitive to the needs of others.

Some pastors and Christian leaders appear to want to be "spiritual dictators" who control their people rather than servants who seek to help others grow. I once heard the pastor of a large church say,"I'm not a dictator, I'm the only tator." How sad to see people become slaves and puppets of a person like this rather than servants of the Lord.

These false teachers, who invaded the Corinthian church were guilty of being dictators. They had attempted to turn the hearts of the people away from Paul, who had sacrificed so much for them (II Corinthians 11). In contrast to this, we

---

see Paul's compassion for the people in not wanting to "pull rank" on them (v. 24). Even though he had great authority as an apostle, he did not want to "lord it over" them. Dictatorial type leadership may produce compliance, but not obedience that comes from wanting to serve the Lord, which is what Paul wanted.

Paul refrained from going to Corinth in person to avoid having to rebuke them and mar the fellowship he had with them in the gospel. Why change joy into sorrow if he could handle this problem through correspondence. Before he reached Corinth in person, he wanted to have the Corinthians problems settled and their questions answered. Then his visit would be positively joyous, and not negatively frustrating.

APPLICATION:

When problems come between Christian brothers it is so easy to want to have our own way so strongly that we destroy the testimony of Christ in the process. Lord, help me to be able to promote a positive spirit among others even when I have to deal with negative things.

II CORINTHIANS

Scripture Reading: 2:5-11

Weekly Memory Verse: 3:5

Topic: Confronting

THOUGHTS ABOUT THE PASSAGE:

"Peace at any price" is not a Biblical principle, for there cannot be true spiritual peace without purity (James 3:13-18). Church discipline is not a popular subject and very few churches today really practice it. Too many churches just sweep things under the rug instead of obeying the Scripture by taking care of the situation in love (Ephesians 4:15).

In the case of the person referred to in this passage, it seems that the church had disciplined him but now that he had repented they refused to forgive him. Paul knows that Satan can and will use this incident to hinder the work of God in the Corinthian church unless it is properly handled. Satan's first objective is to stop the Gospel from going out (4:4). If he can bring disunity to the church, then he has accomplished his objective.

Paul urges the church to forgive the man and gives three basic reasons for this admonition:

1. <u>To forgive him for his own sake</u> (vv. 7-8). The purpose of discipline is not to destroy but to edify and restore.

2. To forgive him for the Lord's sake (vv. 9-10). When others see this unforgiving spirit in Christians they will have a hard time accepting the Lord's forgiveness.
3. To forgive him for the church's sake (v. 11). To harbor bitterness and possessing an unforgiving spirit grieves the Holy Spirit and "gives place to the devil" (Ephesians 4:27-32).

Luther could scarcely bear to pray the Lord's Prayer because his own father had been so stern that the word father painted a picture of grim terror to him. He used to say, "Spare the rod and spoil the child—yes; but, beside the rod keep an apple, to give the child when he has done well." Punishment should encourage and not discourage. In the last analysis, this can happen only when we make it clear that, even when we are punishing a person, we still believe in him.

APPLICATION:

Lord, help me to not be a person who just sweeps wrong doing under the rug, but at the same time I want to always exercise love and concern toward the person being confronted.

II CORINTHIANS

Scripture Reading: 2:12-17

Weekly Memory Verse: 3:5

Topic: Triumph

THOUGHTS ABOUT THE PASSAGE:

It appeared that Paul's plans had completely fallen apart. He had sent Titus to Corinth to find out their spiritual condition and had arranged to meet him in Troas for a first hand report. When Titus failed to show up, Paul became very concerned. For all Paul knew, Titus might have been carrying with him a portion of the Corinthian collection and fallen prey to bandits. He also was very concerned about what was going on in Corinth. Paul had great open doors of ministry at Troas, but he could not concentrate on these because of the circumstances. The circumstances were not comfortable, and Paul could not explain the detours and disappointments, but he was sure God was in control.

Paul now draws attention from himself to the triumphant Christ (v. 14). The picture is that of the "Roman Triumph" parade. When a commander-in-chief won a complete victory over the enemy and gained new territory for the Emperor, he was entitled to a victory parade. In front of his chariot, captives would march carrying incense; their lives were to be spared. Behind him other captives would follow carrying incense; they were to be put to death. The spiritual application is that those who handle the Word of God and make known the gospel share in Christ's victory. The captives in front represent believers giving forth the fragrance of Christ in life. The ones behind the chariot represent other believers who are the fragrance of death, as serving Christ may mean life or death to a lost world around us.

Paul lived not in pessimistic fear, but in the glorious optimism which knew the triumphant life in Christ. There were those who said that he was not fit to preach Christ. There were those who said worse, that he was using the gospel as an excuse to line his own pockets. Again Paul uses the word *eilikrineia* for *purity*. His motives will stand the penetrating rays of the sun. His message is from God, and it will stand the very scrutiny of Christ himself. Paul never feared what men might say, because his conscience told him that he had the approval of God and the "Well done!" of Christ.

APPLICATION:

When things fall apart around me, who do I turn to? The Lord didn't promise me a life with no battles but He has promised to be in the battles with me.

II CORINTHIANS

Scripture Reading: 3:1-3

Weekly Memory Verse: 3:5

Topic: Example

THOUGHTS ABOUT THE PASSAGE:

These legalistic false teachers boasted that they carried "letters of recommendation" from the "important people" in the Jerusalem church. They said, "Where is his letter of recommendation? Does he have a letter of approval from the apostolic council in Jerusalem? If so, let him produce it, otherwise we will just consider him an unauthorized person."

Paul answers these false teachers by saying that it was not necessary for him to have credentials from church leaders. The Corinthians themselves whom he had led to Christ were a visible proof and demonstration of his apostolic effectiveness. They were indeed an epistle, clearly legible to all who were willing to read and understand. It is really sad when a person measures his worth by what people say about him instead of by what God knows about him.

In verse 3, Paul makes a comparison between the law which was written on tables of stone and the gospel which is written in the hearts of men. Even if the Israelites could read these tables of stone, this experience would not change their life. The law is an external thing, and people need an internal power in their lives to be changed. The test of ministry is changed lives and not press releases or statistics.

There is a great truth here; every man is an open letter for Jesus Christ. Every Christian, whether he likes it or not, is an advertisement for Christianity. The honor of Christ is in the hands of his followers. We judge a shopkeeper by the kind of goods he sells, we judge a craftsman by the kind of articles he produces, we judge a Church by the kind of men it creates, and therefore men judge Christ by his followers. Dick Shepard, after years of talking in the open air to people who were outside the Church, declared that he had discovered that "the greatest handicap the Church has is the unsatisfactory lives of professing Christians." When we go out into the world, we have the awe-inspiring responsibility of being open letters, advertisements, for Christ and his Church.

APPLICATION:

As a Christian I may be the only Bible some unsaved folk will ever read! Because of this, I really need to watch my conduct and make sure it is an example that honors Christ.

II CORINTHIANS

Scripture Reading: 3:4-11

Weekly Memory Verse: 5:17

Topic: Spirituality

THOUGHTS ABOUT THE PASSAGE:

The great Boulder Dam scheme in America brought fertility to vast areas which had once been desert. In the making of it there were inevitably those who lost their lives. When the scheme was completed, a tablet was placed into the wall of the dam bearing the names of the workmen who had died, and below stands the inscription: "These died that the desert might rejoice and blossom as the rose." Paul could go through what he did because he knew that it was not in vain; he knew that it was to bring others to Christ. When a man has the conviction that what is happening to him is happening literally for Christ's sake, he can face anything.

Paul was a brilliant and well educated man; yet he did not depend on his own adequacy and gave all the glory to God and not himself. Paul's opponents were legalists who told the people that if they obeyed the law they would become spiritual. This legalistic type of ministry dulled the eyes of the people and made them think they were sufficient in themselves.

Paul goes on to draw a contrast between the covenant of the law granted to Moses and the covenant of the gospel established by Christ. While both the law and the gospel were glorious, they differed radically from each other. Paul did not deny the glory of the Old Testament law but he makes it plain that the New Testament of grace is far superior and he gives the following reasons:

1. Because it brings spiritual life and not death (vv. 7-8). The best the law could do was condemn the sinner but the spirit giveth life.
2. Because it produces changed lives and not just condemnation (vv. 9-10). The law was not given for the purpose of salvation but was like a mirror to help man see his sinful condition.
3. Because it is permanent and not temporary (v. 11). When the Veil in the temple was rent as Christ died on the cross, the law and the Jewish religious system ended (vv. 13-16).

APPLICATION:

It is so easy for me to try to measure spirituality by what I do and what I don't do. My spirituality cannot be measured by whether I go to church every time the doors are open or become a deacon or Sunday school teacher, but by what kind of a person I am on a day to day basis.

II CORINTHIANS

Scripture Reading: 3:12-18

Weekly Memory Verse: 5:17

Topic: Veiled

THOUGHTS ABOUT THE PASSAGE:

The Bible is basically a picture book as it uses illustration after illustration of real life situations to get across to us Biblical principles of life. In this passage we find Paul using the experience of Moses given in Exodus 34:29-35. It tells how Moses' face shone, reflecting the glory of God when he came down from communing with God. However, Moses knew that the glory (just like the Old Testament covenant) would fade away, so he put on a veil. This prevented them from seeing the glory disappear; for after all, who wants to follow a leader who is losing his glory?

It also concealed the Law, which had just been given, because the people were not ready to be told that this system was only temporary. The Jews of Paul's day failed to perceive that the Old Covenant was a preliminary message and preparation for something greater to come. To this very day their minds are still blinded to the finished work of Christ and it is as though the veil upon Moses' face still blinds their hearts (v. 14).

Not only is there a veil which keeps the Jews from seeing the real meaning of Scripture; but there is also a veil which comes between them and God. Sometimes it is the veil of *disobedience*. Very often it is moral and not intellectual blindness which keeps us from seeing God. If we persist in disobeying Him we become less and less capable of seeing Him. Sometimes it is the veil of the *unteachable spirit*. The best teacher on earth cannot teach the man who knows it all already and does not wish to learn. God gave us a free will, and, if we insist upon our own way, we cannot learn His way.

In the Old Covenant when Moses entered the Lord's presence he removed his veil (Exodus 34:34). In the same sense when a Jew (or anyone) turns to the Lord, he must understand and the veil will be removed (v. 16). Then, just as Moses reflected the glory of God, you and I may radiate the glory of God (v. 18). The glory of the Law faded away, but the glory of God's grace should continue to increase in our lives.

APPLICATION:

Is there some area of my life where I still wear a veil? Am I continuing in the old way when I know that all things are to become new? I need to ask the Holy Spirit to remove the veil.

II CORINTHIANS

Scripture Reading: 4:1-6

Weekly Memory Verse: 5:17

Topic: Discouragement

THOUGHTS ABOUT THE PASSAGE:

Larry Olsen describes a man lost in the desert: "He has been out of food and water for days. His lips are swollen, his tongue is swollen, he's all beat up and bloody. Some of his bones are almost peeking through. He has been scraped and beat up by the cactus, sand and sun. He's blistered. As he's crawling over this little hill he comes across this little plant and props himself up on one bloody elbow, looks down at this plant and says, 'You know, if things keep going like this I might get discouraged!'" (*Larry Olsen, Outdoor Survival Skils - Swindoll's Book of Illustrations, p. 164*)

Physically, the demands of the ministry were sometimes almost more than Paul could bear (1:8;11:23-27). However, even more draining were the spiritual demands (7:5;11:28-29). He reflects on these experiences in this passage and tells why, though discouraged at times, he never quit.

One source of discouragement to Paul was the false teachers in the church at Corinth. He was no doubt referring to these Judaizers when he wrote these words (v. 2). Every false teacher claims to base his doctrine on the Word of God, but false teachers handle God's Word in deceptive ways. Satan will do everything in his power to keep lost sinners in the dark and often he uses religious teachers to deceive people. Even today, many of the people who belong to false cults were originally members of Gospel preaching churches.

These Judiazers enjoyed preaching about themselves and bragging about their achievements (10:12-18). They were not servants who tried to help people but instead they were out to take advantage of people. Paul made it plain that the reason he served the church and openly proclaimed the gospel was because of God's work in his life (v. 5). When Paul preached he did not say, "Look at me!" He said, "Look at Jesus Christ, and there you will see the glory of God come to earth in a form that a man can understand." How could he ever get discouraged and quit when he was involved in such a wonderful ministry?

APPLICATION:

When I find myself getting discouraged and wanting to quit, I need to think on what I have in Jesus Christ. Instead of complaining about what I do not have, I need to rejoice in what I do have.

II CORINTHIANS

Scripture Reading: 4:7-18

Weekly Memory Verse: 5:17

Topic: Suffering

THOUGHTS ABOUT THE PASSAGE:

Driving through Texas, a New Yorker collided with a truck carrying a horse. A few months later he tried to collect damages for his injuries. "How can you now claim to have all these injuries?" asked the insurance company's lawyer. "According to the police report, at the time you said you were not hurt." "Look," replied the New Yorker. "I was lying on the road in a lot of pain, and I heard someone say the horse had a broken leg. The next thing I know this Texas Ranger pulls out his gun and shoots the horse. Then he turns to me and asks, 'Are you okay?' (*Reader's Digest, July, 1994, p. 64*).

God has made us the way we are so that we can do the work He wants us to do (v. 7). As a Christian we should never complain because of a lack of gifts or abilities. Each of us is a special vessel made by God for His use. The important thing about a vessel is that it is clean, empty and available. This section is one of three sections in II Corinthians devoted to a listing of Paul's sufferings. Paul was not afraid of suffering because he knew that God controls trials, and God uses trials for His own glory. The natural mind cannot understand this kind of spiritual truth and as a result cannot understand why Christians are victorious in suffering.

Furthermore God never abandons His own. For every trial there is a corresponding encouragement.

After Paul lists some of the trials that were a part of his life and ministry, he shares how God gave him victory over all of them.

   C. He was sure of victory because of Christ's resurrection (v. 14).
   D. He was sure that God would be glorified because all things work together for good (v. 15, Romans 8:28).
   E. He was sure that his trials were working for him, not against him (vv. 16-17).
   F. He was sure that the invisible world was real (v. 18, Hebrews 11:1).

APPLICATION:

How does this chapter make me feel about hard times? How should I act differently because of what I have learned here?

II CORINTHIANS

Scripture Reading: 5:1-9

Weekly Memory Verse: 5:17

Topic: Faith

THOUGHTS ABOUT THE PASSAGE:

A man named Smith was sitting on his roof during a flood, and the water was up to his feet. Before long a fellow in a canoe paddled past and shouted, "Can I give you a lift to higher ground?" "No, thanks," said Smith. "I have faith in the Lord and he will save me." Soon the water rose to Smith's waist. At this point a motorboat pulled up and someone called out, "Can I give you a lift to higher ground?" "No, thanks. I have faith in the Lord and he will save me." Later a helicopter flew by, and Smith was now standing on the roof with water up to his neck. "Grab the rope," yelled the pilot. "I'll pull you up." "No, thanks," said Smith. "I have faith in the Lord and he will save me." But after hours of treading water, poor, exhausted Smith drowned and went to his reward. As he arrived at the Pearly Gates, Smith met his maker and complained about this turn of events. "Tell me, Lord," he said, "I had such faith in you to save me and you let me down. What happened?" To which the Lord replied, "What do you want from me? I sent you two boats and a helicopter!" (*Source Unknown*).

In this passage we find that heaven was not simply a destination for Paul; it was also a motivation. He was anxiously waiting for the day when he would fully participate in the abundant life promised in heaven. He used a tent or earthly house as a picture of our present earthly bodies (v. 1). A tent is a weak, temporary dwelling without much beauty; but our glorified body will be eternal, beautiful, and never show signs of weakness or decay (Philippines 3:20-21). In contrast to the old body, the new body is pictured as a permanent dwelling.

He reminds the Corinthians that the world and its present sufferings are passing away. What is seen (the material) is temporary, but what is unseen (the spiritual) is eternal. No wonder Paul could endure suffering without wavering. His gaze was firmly focused by faith on the Savior and on his heavenly home; not on the seen but on the unseen (v. 7). To live this way is to live by faith and not by sight. Paul had a confident faith that conquered fear, and a future hope that was both a destination and a motivation. Every believer in Jesus Christ has these same marvelous possessions.

APPLICATION:

In our daily walk of life, what does it mean to walk by faith and not by sight? Lord, help me to think of examples our family has experienced of walking by faith!

II CORINTHIANS

Scripture Reading: 5:10-13

Weekly Memory Verse: 5:17

Topic: Judgment

THOUGHTS ABOUT THE PASSAGE:

It appears that Paul is trying to persuade men of his own sincerity. He has no doubt whatever that in the sight of God his hands are clean and his motives pure, but his enemies have cast suspicion on them, and he wishes to demonstrate his sincerity to his Corinthian friends. This is not from any selfish desire to vindicate himself. It is from the knowledge that, if his sincerity is questioned, the impact of his message will be injured. A man's message will always be heard in the context of his character. That is why we need to avoid not only evil, but the very appearance of evil.

A person's eternal destiny will not be determined at the judgment seat of Christ. As a born-again Christian our entrance into heaven was settled at Calvary (John 5:24). However, all believers must one day stand before the "judgment seat of Christ," which will follow the rapture of the church. This "judgment seat" must not be confused with the great white throne judgment which will take place after the millennium and is where Christ will judge the wicked (Revelation 20:11-15). At the "judgment seat of Christ" believers will not have to face their sins but will have to give an account of their works and service for the Lord.

Paul now gives three ways that a Christian may prepare for the judgment seat of Christ:

1. He must maintain a clear conscience (v. 11). As we live and work here on earth, it is easy for us to hide things and pretend, but at the "judgment seat" all things will be revealed. Our motives as well as our works will be exposed.
2. He must not depend on the praise of men (v. 12). The Judaizers in Paul's day loved the praise of men. If we live only for the praise of men we will not win the praise of God.
3. He must ignore the criticism of men (v. 13). Paul was willing to be thought of as a fool. Who would be crazy enough to walk back into a city where he had just been stoned and dragged out, except a person who was utterly devoted to Christ (Acts 14:19-20)?

APPLICATION:

The day is coming when I will stand before the "judgment seat of Christ." Lord, help me to be able to not be ashamed as I give an answer for what I have done in this body.

II CORINTHIANS

Scripture Reading: 5:14-21

Weekly Memory Verse: 5:17

Topic: Salvation

THOUGHTS ABOUT THE PASSAGE:

In verses 14 and 15 Paul comes to two conclusions:

1. The total depravity of man (v.14). If Christ died for all, then all must be dead in trespasses and sin.
2. God's purpose for saving us (v. 15). He died that we might live through Him and for Him, and one day with Him.

In 1858, Francis Ridley Havegal visited Germany with her father, who was being treated for an eye problem. While in a pastor's home, she saw a painting of the crucifixion with words under it that said:"I did this for thee. What has thou done for me?" Quickly she took a piece of paper and wrote a poem based on those words. However, she was not satisfied with it, so she threw the piece of paper into the fireplace. The paper came out unharmed, so her father encouraged her to publish it. Later the famous song writer and composer Phillip Bliss put music to the words and today people all around the world sing it.

I gave My life for thee,
My precious blood I shed,
That thou might'st ransomed be,
And quickened from the dead.
I gave, I gave, My life for thee,
What hast thou given for Me?

In this passage (vv. 16-21) Paul summarizes the motive of the whole Christian life. Christ died for all and the old self of the Christian died in that death. He arose a new man. In this newness of life he has acquired a new set of standards. He no longer judges things by the world's standards.

APPLICATION:

As a Christian, I am Christ's ambassador in this world. Therefore, if sinners reject me and my message, it is Jesus Christ who is actually rejected. What a great privilege it is to serve Him!

II CORINTHIANS

Scripture Reading: 6:1-10

Weekly Memory Verse: 6:14

Topic: Stedfast

THOUGHTS ABOUT THE PASSAGE:

Verse 2 makes it plain that there is no guarantee that any sinner will have the opportunity to be saved tomorrow. There is a story told of a young lady who was arguing that she had plenty of time to accept the Lord. The soul winner handed her a piece of paper and said, "Would you sign a statement that you would be willing to postpone salvation for a year?" "No," she replied. Six months? No, again. One month? She hesitated, and again said no. At that point she could see the folly of her argument because she had no assurance of an opportunity tomorrow, only for today; and she trusted Christ without delay.

Paul paid a tremendous price to be faithful to the ministry God had called him to, and yet it would appear that the Corinthians didn't appreciate all he did for them. In these verses Paul was not begging for praise but he was just reminding the Christians at Corinth that his ministry to them had cost him dearly.

As Paul shares how the pressures were coming in from every side, he lists twenty-seven categories that can be divided as follows:

2. His trials (vv. 4-5).
3. His tools (vv. 6-7).
4. His testimony (vv. 8-10).

In everything he did, Paul always considered what his actions communicated about the Lord. As believers we must minister for Jesus Christ. In the course of each day, non Christians observe us. Paul stood faithful to God whether people praised him or condemned him. He remained active, joyous, and content in the most difficult hardships. As a Christian, we must never let our careless or undisciplined actions be another person's excuse for rejecting Christ.

APPLICATION:

I must never let circumstances or people's expectations govern what I do or don't do in life. I must stand true to God, and refuse to compromise my standards for living regardless of what trials may come into my life.

II CORINTHIANS

Scripture Reading: 6:11-7:1

Weekly Memory Verse: 6:14

Topic: Separation

THOUGHTS ABOUT THE PASSAGE:

It is often argued that we should stay in the midst of churches and bodies whose sins and follies we deplore, in the hope of saving them for God and mankind. Such reasoning has a good deal of force in the first stages of decline. A strong protest may arrest error and stop the gangrene. But as time advances, when the protests have been disregarded, and the arguments trampled underfoot; when the majority have clearly taken up their position against the truth—we have no alternative but to come out and be separate. The place from which we can exert the strongest influence for good is not from within, but from without. Lot lost all influence of his life in Sodom; but Abraham, from the heights of Mamre, was able to exert a mighty influence on its history. (*F. B. Meyer*).

Separation from the ungodly is a basic Bible doctrine. Verses 14 and 15 of this chapter are often applied to various sorts of alliances such as mixed marriages, improper business associations and religious fellowship. The idea of the unequal yoke comes from Deuteronomy 22:10 where it says "Thou shalt not plow with an ox and an ass together." To the Jew an ox was a clean animal and the ass wasn't; and it was wrong to yoke them together (Deuteronomy 14:1-8). Paul is saying that in the same way, it is wrong for believers to be yoked together with unbelievers.

It is unfortunate that this important doctrine of separation has been so misunderstood and abused in recent years. On the one hand some sincerely zealous Christians have turned separation into isolation. They have restricted their association and fellowship to the point where they are fellowshiping in a phone booth and they cannot even get along with themselves. On the other hand, in reaction to this extreme position, other believers have torn down all the walls and will fellowship with anybody, regardless of what he believes or how he lives. We must remember that separation is not just a negative act but it is also a positive act of dedication to God. In our desire for doctrinal and personal purity, we must not isolate ourselves from those who desperately need our ministry and the Word of God.

APPLICATION:

In light of Paul's counsel, what relationships with others, if any, do I need to change? I must be sure that I am always turning away from sin, not people, and turning to God in everything I do.

II CORINTHIANS

Scripture Reading: 7:2-7

Weekly Memory Verse: 6:14

Topic: Rejoicing

THOUGHTS ABOUT THE PASSAGE:

Oliver Wendell Holmes, Jr., was a member of the U.S. Supreme Court for 30 years. His mind, wit and work earned him the unofficial title of "the greatest justice since John Marshall." At one point in his life, Justice Holmes explained his choice of a career by saying: "I might have entered the ministry if certain clergymen I knew had not looked and acted so much like undertakers." (*Moody Bible Institute's Today In The Word, June, 1988, p. 13.*).

In this passage Paul resumed the story that he left in 2:13, where he said he went to Macedonia to look for Titus. Though Paul still had many problems and hardships to face, he found comfort and joy in the ministry God had given to him. Titus had visited the Corinthian church and now he rejoins Paul in Macedonia (vv. 5-6). His report brings rejoicing to the apostle's heart. The church had received Titus and now they were ready to receive Paul (v. 13). He asks them to trust him, for he had never done anything to wrong them.

Paul's frame of mind, before Titus' arrival was far fr~ being at peace. It says that "he had no rest" (v. 5) ~

apostle Paul was not always on a spiritual high and he was not afraid to admit it. His conflicts, fears and depression were brought on by opposition and persecution in Macedonia. He also was not sure how Titus was being treated by the Corinthians and how they had responded to his letter.

Did you ever wonder why it is often so difficult to assure people of your love? What more could Paul do to convince them? He was willing to die for them if necessary and at every opportunity that he had he was bragging about them to others and yet they had been criticizing him (v. 4). Now, the Corinthians had evidenced to Titus a repentant spirit and a desire to be reconciled to Paul, for this he was rejoicing (v. 7).

APPLICATION:

There is joy in seeing someone we love being welcomed and well-treated. What is true of us is true of God. That is why I can best show my love for God by loving other people. The thing that delights the heart of God is to see one of his children kindly treated.

II CORINTHIANS

Scripture Reading: 7:8-16

Weekly Memory Verse: 6:14

Topic: Rebuke

THOUGHTS ABOUT THE PASSAGE:

John Wesley and a preacher-friend of plain habits were once invited to dinner where the host's daughter, noted for her beauty, had been profoundly impressed by Wesley's preaching. During a pause in the meal, Wesley's friend took the young woman's hand and called attention to the sparkling rings she wore. "What do you think of this, sir, for a Methodist hand?" The girl turned crimson. Wesley likewise was embarrassed, for his aversion to jewelry was only too well known. But with a benevolent smile, he simply said, "The hand is very beautiful." Wesley's remark both cooled the too-hot water poured by his friend, and made the foot-washing gentle. The young woman appeared at the evening service without her jewels, and became a strong Christian. (*Source unknown*).

One of the most difficult things to do in life is to rebuild a shattered relationship. Unfortunately, there are many broken relationships today in homes, churches and ministries, which can only be repaired when people face problems honestly and deal with them Biblically and lovingly.

This is what Paul is trying to do in II Corinthians

169

especially in chapters 6 and 7. Paul had written a very severe letter of rebuke to the Corinthians and at times had regretted it (v. 8). His primary motive in writing the letter was to benefit them. They had read his "painful letter," had repented of their sins and disciplined the members who had created the problems. Now, Paul's heart rejoiced that they had accepted his message and had acted upon it (v. 9). He had suffered a great deal because of this situation but this made all of his efforts worthwhile.

In Paul's discussions with Titus, he was convinced that the opposition in Corinth came only from a small group of dissenters and the vast majority of the congregation wanted to do what was right. Now this conviction is confirmed by the report Titus gives to Paul.

APPLICATION:

I must never let pride keep me from admitting sin in my life. I must accept correction as a tool for my Spiritual growth and do all I can to correct problems that are pointed out to me.

II CORINTHIANS

Scripture Reading: 8:1-6

Weekly Memory Verse: 6:14

Topic: Offering

THOUGHTS ABOUT THE PASSAGE:

Paul writing from Macedonia, hoped that news of the generosity of these churches would encourage the Corinthian believers and motivate them to solve their problems and unite the fellowship. He is usually thought of as being a great theologian and missionary. However, what is often not known about him is that he was also a financial genius of the early church. Chapters 8 and 9 of this epistle concern the offering for the poor saints at Jerusalem.

One of the things Paul had been organizing for several years and which he majored on in his third missionary journey was the taking up of this special "relief offering." Early in his ministry he had promised to remember the poor and he wanted to keep that promise (Galatians 2:6-10). But he also hoped to accomplish a couple of other things. He was trusting that the generosity of the Gentiles would silence the jealousy of the Jews, and at the same time, the unity of the Gentile churches would be strengthened as they shared with the Jewish congregations across the sea.

The point of giving is not so much the amount we give, but why and how we give. God does not want gifts giv grudgingly. Instead, He wants us to give as these churches did; out of dedication to Christ, love for fellow believers, the joy of helping those in need, and the fact that it was simply the good and right thing to do. Paul stressed the fact that giving is more blessed than receiving and he shares the following evidences that will appear when our giving is motivated by grace.

- <u>When we give in spite of circumstances</u> (vv. 1-2). Paul uses the Macedonian churches as an example. They were in poverty and yet they gave.
- <u>When we give enthusiastically</u> (vv. 3-4). It is possible to give generously but not with enthusiasm. The Macedonian churches even begged to be included.
- <u>When we give as Christ gave</u> (vv. 5-6). The Macedonian Christians gave themselves to God and others. If we give ourselves to God, we will have little problem in giving to God.

APPLICATION:

I need to make sure that my motives for giving are right. It should never be because I have to give but because I want to give and with a joyful heart.

II CORINTHIANS

Scripture Reading: 8:7-15

Weekly Memory Verse: 6:14

Topic: Money

THOUGHTS ABOUT THE PASSAGE:

I have known pastors, missionaries and Bible school students who argue that since they devote their whole life to serving the Lord, they are not obligated to give financially to the Lord's work. In verses 7 and 8 Paul says just the opposite is true. If you are wonderfully gifted from God, you ought to want to give more.

These Corinthian believers were so wrapped up in the gifts of the Spirit that they neglected the grace of giving. They had an abundance of spiritual gifts and yet they were lax in keeping their promise and sharing in the collection. Paul had every right to expect the Corinthian church to partici-pate in this special offering. This was their expressed desire more than a year before this. He is only asking that they follow through with their original commitment. How easy it is to make a commitment to support some missionary or project and then not follow through. How disappointing it must be to our Lord to see an individual or church promise to support a missionary and then when he gets out on the mission field they drop him.

Dr. Charles Ryrie in his teaching on this book says that we

should study "Faith Promise" giving in the context of verse 12, where it states that a gift "is accepted according to that a man hath, and not according to that he hath not." The whole emphasis of "Faith Promise" giving is that we don't promise to give something that we have, but instead promise to give something that we don't have. Then we will trust the Lord to provide. Our giving needs to be in proportion to our income.

Three Levels of Giving:

1. You have to. (law)
2. You ought to. (obligation)
3. You want to. (grace)

APPLICATION:

I need to be a good steward by example. I will look for opportunities to teach others how they can give to the Lord's work if they just trust the Lord to meet their needs instead of going into debt.

II CORINTHIANS

Scripture Reading: 8:16-24

Weekly Memory Verse: 6:14

Topic: Stewardship

THOUGHTS ABOUT THE PASSAGE:

A man had a heart attack and was rushed to the hospital. He could receive little company and was to avoid excitement. While in the hospital a rich uncle died and left him a million dollars. His family wondered how to break the news to him with the least amount of excitement. It was decided to ask the preacher if he would go and break the news quietly to the man. The preacher gradually led up to the question. The preacher asked the patient what he would do if he inherited a million dollars. He said, "I think I would give half of it to the church." The preacher dropped dead. (*Source unknown*).

One of the things in Christian circles that tends to be done in a careless manner is the handling of money. The apostle Paul in this passage organizes the collection of funds for the saints in Jerusalem so that it will be managed honestly and faithfully. We can find here the qualifications for people handling funds in a local church or Christian organization:

- A desire to serve (vv. 16-17) - Titus had a desire to help in the gathering of this special offering and was not just put on this Finance Committee because no one else would do it.

- A burden for lost souls (v. 18) - We do not know who this brother was but we are told that he had a desire to share the gospel. Every Finance Committee needs to have members who have a burden for lost souls.
- A desire to honor God (v. 19) - When a church selects deacons or elders, to handle the "spiritual affairs" of the church, and trustees to handle the "material and financial affairs," it is making an unbiblical distinction. One of the most spiritual things a church can do is use its money wisely for spiritual ministry.
- A reputation for honesty (vv. 20-22) - It is very unwise for anyone to handle funds in a Christian organization by himself. There needs to be at least two and preferably three people who collect and count it in order to avoid any accusations.
- A cooperative spirit (vv. 23-24) - Finance Committee members do not own the money. It belongs to the Lord and they just manage it.

APPLICATION:

Of the qualifications mentioned above which ones do I need to work on the most?

II CORINTHIANS

Scripture Reading: 9:1-5

Weekly Memory Verse: 9:6

Topic: Commitment

THOUGHTS ABOUT THE PASSAGE:

W. A. Criswell tells of an ambitious young man who told his pastor he'd promised God a tithe of his income. They prayed for God to bless his career. At that time he was making $40.00 per week and tithing $4.00. In a few years his income increased and he was tithing $500.00 per week. He called on the pastor to see if he could be released from his tithing promise. It was too costly now. The pastor replied, "I don't see how you can be released from your promise, but we can ask God to reduce your income to $40.00 a week, then you'd have no problem tithing $4.00." (*W. A. Criswell, A Guidebook for Pastors, p. 156*).

Why is it that Christians often need to be motivated to give when God has given us so much? God had provided for the Corinthians in such a wonderful way and yet they were hesitant to share what they had with others. One year before this, the Corinthians had enthusiastically said they would share in this offering for the needy saints. Paul had used this zeal of the Corinthians to challenge the Macedonians. The Macedonians had followed through on their promise, but up to this point the Corinthians had done nothing. Since there were special representatives from the Macedonian churches on this financial committee, Paul was concerned that his boasting might not be in vain (Acts 20:4). It would not only be an embarrassment to the apostle but a disgrace to themselves if they did not keep their promise.

While he applies pressure, he tactfully suggests that he is only concerned that they be on schedule (v. 3). Apparently Paul did not see anything wrong or unspiritual about asking people to give. He did not tell them how much to give, but he did expect them to keep their promise. If it is acceptable to make financial commitments for telephones, credit cards etc. then it certainly ought to be O.K. to make commitments for the work of the Lord. Then these commitments should be kept, just the same as the one for our telephone.

APPLICATION:

God has blessed me financially and materially so that I can give to the needs of others. This means that I need to be alert to the needs of others and be faithful in fulfilling my commitments.

II CORINTHIANS

Scripture Reading: 9:6-15

Weekly Memory Verse: 9:6

Topic: Generosity

THOUGHTS ABOUT THE PASSAGE:

L. Kraft, head of the Kraft Cheese Corp., who had given approximately 25% of his enormous income to Christian causes for many years, said, "The only investment I ever made which has paid consistently increasing dividends is the money I have given to the Lord." (*W. A. Criswell, A Guidebook for Pastors, p. 154*).

In these verses Paul points out principles found in the Word of God as well as those drawn from experience to show why and how we are to give.

1. The givers are blessed (vv. 6-10).
2. The receivers needs are met (vv. 11-12).
3. The Lord receives glory (vv. 13-15).

Warren Wiersbe says, "Giving is not something we do, but something we are." When the material things of life are placed first, God is usually excluded, but when the "kingdom of God" is placed first (Matthew 6:33), God sees to it that all of our needs are met (Philippians 4:19). The following principles of life can be seen in this passage:

- <u>We reap what we sow</u> (v. 6) - Just as the more seed a farmer sows, the better chance he will have for a bigger harvest; the more we invest in the Lord's work, the more "fruit" will abound to our account (Philippians 4:10-20).
- <u>We reap as we sow with right motives</u> (v. 7) - Whether the farmer's motive for reaping is money, pleasure or pride makes very little difference. However, the Christian's motive for giving is very important and God cannot bless the giver unless his heart is right.
- <u>We reap even while we are sowing</u> (vv. 8-11) - The farmer has to wait for his harvest, but the believer begins to reap a harvest immediately as he invests in the Lord's work.

APPLICATION:

I need to consider if I am a generous sower or is it something I do reluctantly. I always need to be looking for opportunities to get the gospel out.

II CORINTHIANS

Scripture Reading: 10:1-6

Weekly Memory Verse: 9:6

Topic: Warfare

THOUGHTS ABOUT THE PASSAGE:

A custom of the natives in New Guinea is told. At certain times they have rituals, songs, and dances. They work themselves up into a frenzy and the ritual culminates in what are called "the murder songs," in which they shout before God the names of the people they wish to kill. When the natives became Christian, they retained these customs and that ritual, However, in the murder songs, they no longer shouted the names of the people they hated, but the names of the *sins* they hated, and called on God to destroy them. An old pagan custom had been captured for Christ. (*Source Unknown*)

We need to keep in mind that throughout this letter Paul is writing to a divided church, and a church that is being seduced by false teachers. These false teachers charged Paul with being very courageous when he wrote letters from a distance, but said that he was very weak when he was present with the Corinthians. I remember a few years ago of hearing a great Christian leader of our day described as a person who had a poison pen when he wrote, but was like a gentle lamb when you heard him preach. If Paul was a weakling, then so was Jesus Christ; for Jesus was very meek and gentle (Matthew 11:29). However, our Lord could also be stern and even showed anger when the occasion demanded it (Matthew 15:1-2).

In this section of his letter, Paul confronts these false teachers and charges them with being ministers of Satan who want to destroy the work of God. Like many "religious personalities" today, these Judaizers impressed the people with their overpowering personalities. As you read these verses you could get the impression that Paul was bragging about himself; but such was not the case. His purpose was to exalt Christ and not himself (I Corinthians 2:1-5). Christians usually reflect the atmosphere of the church or fellowship they are associated with. If they are in an atmosphere of dictatorial leadership, they will depend on man's wisdom and strength. If they are in an atmosphere of humility and love, they will learn to depend on the Lord. Paul wanted his converts to trust the Lord and not the servant, so he had deliberately "played down" his own authority and ability.

APPLICATION:

As a Christian I need to "cast down imaginations and everything that exalts itself against the knowledge of God and bring into captivity every thought to the obedience of Christ" (v. 5).

II CORINTHIANS

Scripture Reading: 10:7-12

Weekly Memory Verse: 9:6

Topic: Consistent

THOUGHTS ABOUT THE PASSAGE:

"A man's life is always more forcible than his speech. When men take stock of him they reckon his deeds as dollars and his words as pennies. If his life and doctrine disagree, the mass of onlookers accept his practice and reject his preaching." (*C.H. Spurgeon*).

The Corinthians looked only on the surface of things and as a result the false apostles found them to be gullible (v. 7). They interpreted Paul's love and meekness as a sign of weakness. These false teachers were accusing Paul of not being a true apostle, for if he was, he would show it by using his authority. The big difference between Paul and the Judaizers was that Paul used his authority to build up the church, while the Judiazers used the church to build up their authority. It is sort of like churches today that use people to build their church rather than using the church to build people.

In the economy of God, position and power are not an evidence of true authority. In fact, Jesus warned his followers that they were not to pattern their leadership after the Gentiles who loved to "lord it over" others as they tried to act important. How a Christian uses authority is an evidence

183

of his spiritual maturity and character. An immature person demands respect while a mature person earns it. The key is to be a leader and not a boss. The boss says "Go" while the leader says "Let's go." The boss knows how it is to be done but the leader shows how it is to be done.

Paul does not measure his credentials as his enemies do,"measuring themselves by themselves" (v. 12). He says that a person who does so is not wise. Our standard of measurement should come from the Word of God. It is easy enough to say, "I am as good as the next man," and it may be true. But the point is, are we as good as Jesus Christ? He is our true rod of measurement and our proper standard of comparison: When we measure ourselves by Him, there is no room left for pride. "Self-praise," says Paul, "is no honor." It is not his own, but Christ's "Well done!" that man must seek.

APPLICATION:

I need to be careful that I do not want to compare my test scores and achievements in life with those of other people. This is what Paul is warning against. One of the biggest stumbling blocks of people coming to the Lord is their saying they are not as bad as someone else.

II CORINTHIANS

Scripture Reading: 10:13-18

Weekly Memory Verse: 9:6

Topic: Boasting

THOUGHTS ABOUT THE PASSAGE:

Paul poses three questions that we may ask ourselves as we seek to measure our ministries:

- <u>Am I where God wants me to be</u>? (vv. 13-14) - God is not going to measure us by the gifts and opportunities that he gave to D.L. Moody or Jack Wyrtzen but by our own work. Paul was assigned to go to the Gentiles and he was to go where no other apostle had ministered (Acts 9:15). He was not trying to duplicate the work of others and neither should we.
- <u>Is God glorified by my ministry</u>? (vv. 15-17) - The Corinthians were prone to glory in men. When they heard the report of what these Judiazers had done and saw the letters of recommendation that they had, they were very impressed. In comparison, Paul and his ministry looked small and unsuccessful. We must remember that the final test is not when the reports are published for the annual meeting but at the Judgment Seat of Christ. If men get the glory, then God cannot be glorified.
- <u>Can the Lord commend my work</u>? (v. 18) - How does God show His approval of our work? It usually

185

comes through testing. He permits difficulties to come in order that our work may be tested and approved. This may come through financial losses, physical hardships or spiritual battles. Whether we fall apart or grow stronger in each situation shows whether God can commend our work or not.

Whenever anybody boasts, Paul says, it is to be in what the Lord has done: "But he that glorieth, let him glory in the Lord. For not he that commendeth himself is approved, but whom the Lord commendeth" (vv. 17-18). This certainly wipes out, with one stroke, all the proud evaluations you see men making of their own ministries. You never hear that from Paul. He recognized that the only thing that counts is what Christ does in him, not what he does for Christ. Anytime he talks about what he has done he does it with apologies. He only does it because that is the kind of argument these Corinthians have been listening to from false teachers.

APPLICATION:

I want to be able to answer the three questions above in a positive way as it applies to my life. I do not want my life to be spent on myself but on the things that will count for Christ and eternity.

II CORINTHIANS

Scripture Reading: 11:1-9

Weekly Memory Verse: 9:6

Topic: Distortion

THOUGHTS ABOUT THE PASSAGE:

In the final chapters of Second Corinthians, the Apostle Paul is dealing with probably the most powerful tool, the most dangerous threat to a church the devil has – infiltration – the destruction of a church from within by teachers who are straying from the truth. This is still a dangerous threat to churches today. They are being destroyed from within by the satanic process of *infiltration*, by people who come in and gradually began to teach a deviate gospel. That is what was happening here at Corinth, and that is what is threatening many of our churches today.

In this passage we find Paul comparing himself to a "spiritual father" caring for his family. The picture is of a loving daughter engaged to be married. The engaged woman owes her love and allegiance to the one she is engaged to. If she was to share her heart with any other man she would be guilty of unfaithfulness. A divided heart leads to a defiled life and a destroyed relationship. Born again Christians are the bride waiting for the bridegroom to return and need to be faithful to Him.

Paul is comparing the church in Corinth to Eve. Instead of

187

resisting the devil's lead to disobedience Eve listened and gave in. He says the devil's representatives in Corinth are doing the very same things as they make this threefold appeal:

1. They claimed to be associated with the twelve apostles.
2. They claimed to have superiority in speaking abilities.
3. They claimed their method of being supported by the churches was proof of authority.

Paul sacrificed in order to minister to the church at Corinth. While there, he labored with his own hands as a tent maker (Acts 18:1-3) and even received gifts from other churches so that he might evangelize Corinth. He did this so no one could accuse him of using the preaching of the Gospel as a means of making money. A loving father does not lay his burdens on his children but instead he sacrifices so that the children might have what they need.

APPLICATION:

I need to be careful that I do not give more importance to associations, speaking abilities and methods than I do to faithfulness to the Lord and commitment to His Word.

II CORINTHIANS

Scripture Reading: 11:10-15

Weekly Memory Verse: 9:6

Topic: Infiltration

THOUGHTS ABOUT THE PASSAGE:

Paul had taught these people the principle that he who preaches the gospel has a right to live by the gospel. It was he who taught them the old proverb, "Thou shalt not muzzle the ox that treads the corn" (Deut. 25:4). Yet when he came to Corinth he would not accept any support from anybody. He wanted to demonstrate in his own life that the gospel is free-of-charge. Because of this these teachers in Corinth were saying, "You know the reason why Paul isn't supported by you? It is because he is an amateur apostle. He is not a professional one like us."

Up to this point Paul has been dealing graciously with his enemies, but now he lays everything on the table and says what he really thinks of them. "For such are false apostles, deceitful workers, transforming themselves into the apostles of Christ" (v. 13). Who are these false apostles? We cannot be absolutely sure but several factors suggest that they were Palestinian Jews and members of the Jerusalem church. One of the things that points to this is that they carried letters of commendation from the church, possibly under the auspices of the Jerusalem Council (II Corinthians 3:1). That they were self-appointed teachers to enforce Mosiac ordinances is certain (Acts 15:24).

It is interesting to note that Paul did not contest their appeal to be under the authority of the "super-apostles" (Jerusalem council). But he did refute the value of such an appeal and stated that this was a matter of human association rather than proof of divine accreditation. It is really no surprise that these false teachers have been able to deceive the Corinthian believers,"for Satan himself is transformed into an angel of light" (v. 14). Like whitewashed tombs, they may have looked righteous but inside there was only death and decay (Matthew 23:27-28). One day their true character will be revealed and their judgment will be according to their works (v. 15).

APPLICATION:

I want to be able to recognize a false teacher if he presents himself as an angel of light. Then I must be able to warn other believers about false teachers who try to infiltrate the Church.

II CORINTHIANS

Scripture Reading: 11:16-21

Weekly Memory Verse: 13:5

Topic: Boasting

THOUGHTS ABOUT THE PASSAGE:

A sightseeing bus was making the rounds through Washington, D. C., and the driver was pointing out spots of interest. As they passed the Pentagon building, he mentioned that it cost taxpayers millions of dollars and that it took a year and a half to build. A little old woman piped up: "In Peoria we could have built the same building for less, and it would have been completed even sooner than that!" The next sight on the tour was the Justice Department building. Once again the bus driver said that it cost so many millions to build and took almost two years to complete. The woman repeated: "In Peoria we would have done it for less money, and it would have been finished much sooner." The tour finally came to the Washington Monument, and the driver passed by without saying a word. The old woman shouted to the driver, "What's that back there?" The driver looked out the window, waited a minute and then said, "Search me, lady. It wasn't there yesterday." (*Source unknown*).

What Paul is about to do in this passage is contrary to his character. He never had any problem boasting about Christ and telling of His sufferings, but he was always hesitant to speak of his own painful experience as a servant of the Lord.

However, because the spiritual welfare of a congregation in danger of being led astray is at stake, he feels it is necessary to write about himself and boast in his experiences (v. 16). In verse 17 Paul is not denying the inspiration of his words but instead he is admitting that, by boasting, he was being very unlike the Lord. However, he felt that he had to do it to prove his love for the Corinthians and to protect them from those attempting to lead them astray.

Paul seems to be saying, since boasting is the "in thing" in your fellowship, then I will boast. Perhaps he had the principle of Proverbs 26:5 in mind where it says: "Answer a fool according to his folly, lest he be wise in his own conceit." These false teachers did not seem to be ashamed to boast in order to help themselves and to get what they could out of the church. Paul, on the contrary, was boasting so that he might help the church. Up to this point, the Corinthians thought that Paul's meekness was weakness, and that these false teachers' arrogance was power.

APPLICATION:

It is much better for me to seek the praise of God rather than the praise of people.

II CORINTHIANS

Scripture Reading: 11:22-33

Weekly Memory Verse: 13:5

Topic: Suffering

THOUGHTS ABOUT THE PASSAGE:

The only survivor of a shipwreck washed up on a small uninhabited island. He cried out to God to save him, and every day he scanned the horizon for help, but none seemed forthcoming. Exhausted, he eventually managed to build a rough hut and put his few possessions in it. But one day, after hunting for food, he arrived home to find his little hut in flames, the smoke rolling up to the sky. The worst had happened; he was stung with grief. Early the next day, though, a ship drew near the island and rescued him. "How did you know I was here?" he asked the crew. "We saw your smoke signal," they replied. Though it may not seem so now, your present difficulty may be instrumental to your future happiness. (*John Yates, Falls Church, Virginia, quoted in Leadership, Winter Quarter, 1992*).

Some of Paul's religious assailants in Corinth were no doubt Jews. They hurled the charge at Paul that he was no true Hebrew. They said he had apostatized from the faith and that he could not possibly be a faithful minister of God. With this in mind, Paul proceeds to describe his own experiences and consecration to God.

First he insists that he is indeed an Israelite and a genuine minister (vv. 21-23). Then he launches into a description of his personal experiences as an apostle. As examples of dedication and privilege his list include dangers, pain, and pressures from all sides (v. 26-28). Paul ended this narration of his sufferings by telling of his humiliating experience at Damascus, where he was smuggled out of the city in a basket and let down over the wall (vv. 32-33).

While it is true that any traveler could have suffered these things, Paul endured them because of his love for Christ and for the Christians. We cannot help but admire the courage and devotion of the Apostle Paul. Each trial left its mark on his life, and yet he just kept moving on, serving the Lord. If the Lord places you in a position of leadership and authority, remember Paul's kind of empathy and concern for people.

APPLICATION:

The trials and hurts I experience will build character in my life, demonstrate my faith in the Lord and prepare me to further serve Him.

II CORINTHIANS

Scripture Reading: 12:1-10

Weekly Memory Verse: 13:5

Topic: Grace

THOUGHTS ABOUT THE PASSAGE:

To seek to earn, merit, or purchase salvation is to insult the Giver. Imagine yourself invited to a banquet in the White House by the president of the United States. You are seated at a table that is filled with the choist foods. Every effort is made to give you a most enjoyable evening. At the end of a lovely visit, the president stands at the door to bid you good-bye. What do you do? As you leave do you press a dime into his hand and say, "Thank you very much for your kindness. I realize it has cost you a lot of money, and I want to help you pay for the meal." Is that the proper response to his kindness? On the contrary, it would be a very rude and insulting gesture. So it would be with God's grace. (*William MacDonald, The Grace of God - Swindoll's Book of Illustrations, p. 250.*)

In the previous chapter Paul's focus of attention has been on earthly, physical experiences in the gospel. Now he shifts his attention to two experiences he has had from God. In order to avoid exalting himself he describes these experiences in the third person.

    1. <u>The revelation</u> (vv. 1-6) - Fourteen years before the

writing of this letter Paul had been caught up into the very presence of Christ in heaven (v. 20). Paul was not quite sure whether God had taken him bodily to heaven, or whether his spirit had left his body. Possibly this was when he was stoned and his broken and bruised body lay in the dust near Lystra (Acts 14:19). At any rate Paul had kept quiet about this experience for 14 years. If he had been seeking honor for himself, he would have immediately told what had happened and would have become famous. Instead, he exercised discipline and told his experience to no one.

2. The thorn in the flesh (vv. 7-10) - The Lord knows how to balance our lives. If we have only victories and blessings, we may become proud; so He permits us to have burdens as well. For this reason he permitted his dear apostle to have a "thorn in the flesh." We do not know what it was except that it was some annoying, painful and persistent source of suffering. Some Bible scholars think it was an eye affliction of some kind (Galatians 6:11). Three times Paul asked the Lord to remove it but instead He just gave him the grace to endure it. An acrostic of the word grace is God's Riches Available at Christ's Expense.

APPLICATION:

God did not give Paul any explanations but instead gave him His grace. When I face obstacles, it is only by His grace and His power that I will be made effective to do a work that has everlasting value.

II CORINTHIANS

Scripture Reading: 12:11-18

Weekly Memory Verse: 13:5

Topic: Motive

THOUGHTS ABOUT THE PASSAGE:

H. L. Gee somewhere tells of a tramp who came begging to a good woman's door. She went to get something to give him and found that she had no change in the house. She went to him and said, "I have not a penny of small change. I need a loaf of bread. Here is a pound note. Go and buy the loaf and bring me back the change and I will give you something." The man executed the commission and returned and she gave him a small coin. He took it with tears in his eyes. "It's not the money," he said, "it's the way you trusted me. No one ever trusted me like that before, and I can't thank you enough." It is easy to say that the woman took a risk that only a soft-hearted fool would take, but she had given that man more than money. She had given him something of herself by giving her trust. (*Source Unknown*).

Apparently the false teachers in Corinth were suggesting that Paul's unwillingness to accept support from the church was simply a coverup. They thought that he really had a love for money, and the offering he claimed to be taking for the suffering saints in Jerusalem was only going to be used to fill his own pockets. Also his reason for sending Titus ahead was to insure financial gain for himself. With this in mind, Paul wanted to set the record straight. In fact he found it very disappointing that they charged him and his associates with underhanded self-gratification. He attempts to prove that his motive is right for the sake of the gospel and not to satisfy his own ego, in the following two ways:

2. His previous behavior (vv. 13-16) - When he had visited them before he had refused to be a burden to them and had supported himself with his own hands and through the love gifts from other churches. He had never begged for himself, only for others.
3. The behavior of his associates (vv. 17-18). None of his associates that came to help them tried to exploit or take advantage of them. Titus simply walked in Paul's steps and was motivated by love for them and not personal gain.

APPLICATION:

When I am falsely accused, I should not think only about saving my own reputation but I should be more concerned about what people will think about Christ.

II CORINTHIANS

Scripture Reading: 12:19-21

Weekly Memory Verse: 13:5

Topic: Divisions

THOUGHTS ABOUT THE PASSAGE:

The writing of this letter was to pave the way for Paul's coming to Corinth. Therefore this letter was to correct any moral or spiritual abuses which still lingered in the Corinthian assembly. He made it clear that sins in the church must be dealt with in a Biblical way. To "sweep them under the rug"only makes matters worse. Sin in the church is like cancer in the human body and it must be cut out.

The sins Paul mentions in this passage are either the result of church division or caused by lax morality which disunity tends to produce (vv. 20-21). Legalism and immorality are often frequent bedfellows (Philippians 3:3,19). If you don't believe this is true, just look at the great number of legalistic churches today where the pastor or someone on staff has gotten involved in immorality with someone in the church. Then, this sin is often just "swept under the rug" by others.

Paul lists what might be called the 11 marks of the "unchristian" Church. (1) There are (1) *debates* that denote rivalry and discord about place and prestige; (2) *envyings* which are the desire to have what is not ours to have. There are

(3) outbursts of *wrath* which denote sudden explosions of passionate anger that sweep a man into doing things for which afterwards he is bitterly sorry; (4) *strife* which describes that utterly selfish and self-centered ambition which is in everything for what it can get out of it for itself. There are (5) *backbitings* and (6) *whisperings*. The first word describes the open, loud-mouthed attack, the insults flung out in public, against those whose views are different. The second is a much nastier word which describes the whispering campaign of malicious gossip. There are (7) *swellings* (conceits) where a man magnifies himself when he should magnify his office; (8) *tumults* which is the word for disorders and anarchy. Finally there are the sins of which even yet some of the Corinthians may not have repented. There is *(9) uncleanness* which describes the life muddied with wallowing in the world's ways and (10) *fornication* as when people did not regard adultery as a sin and expected a man to take his pleasures where he could. Then there was (11) *lasciviousness* (uncleanness) that knows no restraint, that has no sense of the decencies of things.

APPLICATION:

I must live differently than unbelievers, not letting secular society dictate how I am to treat others.

II CORINTHIANS

Scripture Reading: 13:1-10

Weekly Memory Verse: 13:5

Topic: Self Examination

THOUGHTS ABOUT THE PASSAGE:

As we come to the last chapter of this Corinthian letter most of the church has repented and changed its attitude toward Paul. However, there is a handful of people who are still following the false teachers and living in a worldly manner and open immorality. It is with this in mind that Paul faces them with one final question in verse 5 which is the key to this passage. "Examine yourselves, whether you be in the faith, prove your own selves. Know ye not your own selves, how that Christ is in you, except ye be reprobates?" The question is not whether you believe the truth, but whether you are in the truth. It is possible to know about Christ on Calvary and yet know nothing about Christ in the heart. Christ on Calvary will save no man, unless Christ is in the heart. The bottom line is, can you say that Jesus Christ is in you? If not, you are lost and on your way to a Christless eternity.

Paul turns the focus to them as he says, "Examine yourselves, you have disputed my doctrine; examine whether you be in the faith. You have made me prove my apostleship; prove your own selves. Use the powers which you have been so wrongfully exercising upon me to test your own character. When you answer the question about yourself, you will also know that I am a real apostle" (v. 6). He explains that he is not looking for an opportunity to come and demonstrate his authority as an apostle by judging them, but what he wants is their moral improvement (vv. 7-9).

In verse 10, he emphasizes a principle that is often forgotten today. He makes it clear that true authority is never intended to destroy people or tear them down, but it is to build them up. In other words, it is not given so that somebody can lord it over their brothers. Yet in many churches today the pastor's role is that he is in authority in the church and in essence he is "the pope." In our early days in the ministry we found ourselves associated with a group that wanted to exercise control over every area of our life, even to the point of telling us who we could have as guests in our home and who we could talk to and not talk to. When we left them, the pastor attempted to assassinate our character in any way he could, but the Lord prevailed and continued to bless our lives in His ministry.

APPLICATION:

I am so thankful that as I examine myself in the faith I can say that Christ lives in me.

II CORINTHIANS

Scripture Reading: 13:11-14

Weekly Memory Verse: 13:5

Topic: Unity

THOUGHTS ABOUT THE PASSAGE:

In the church there is a bond of family, yet room for variety. The devil tries to disrupt unity. To chickens tied at the legs and thrown over a clothesline may be united, but they do not have unity. (*Leslie Flynn, Great Church Fights - Swindoll's Book of Illustrations, p. 599*)

Paul's final appeal in this letter is a call for unity. In the first nine chapters he addressed the majority of the Christians in the Corinthian assembly. In chapters 10 - 13:10, his words were directed primarily to those who questioned his integrity. In fact, he is not even certain if these are true believers. But now in his closing statement the apostle turns his attention once again to those who really love and appreciate him, as he calls them "brethren" (v. 11). The apostle sees beyond all the fragmentation in Corinth to the basic unity of the church. God created that unity. Christians belong to each other. They are part of the family of God and Paul says they ought to act that way.

Paul now summons these Corinthians to be mature, content, and in unity, which has not been a characteristic of the Corinthian assembly. He urges them to enter into the comfort of the Lord and reminds them of the availability of divine love and peace. Such unity was to be exhibited with a "holy kiss." Since ancient times this kiss has been a form of greeting and a gesture of love and fellowship. However, it was usually exchanged between members of the same sex.

In closing, the saints with whom Paul was staying at the time he wrote I Corinthians send their greetings (v. 13). Paul also included the blessing of the triune God so that the grace manifested by the Son, the love expressed by the Father, and the fellowship created by the Holy Spirit might be experienced in Corinth (v. 14). This is one of the clearest references to the Trinity found in the New Testament.

APPLICATION:

As a Christian, if I am depending on the grace of our Lord Jesus Christ, walking in the love of God, participating in the fellowship of the Holy Spirit, and not walking in the flesh, I will be a part of the solution and not a part of the problem. That is the kind of a Christian I want to be.

WEEKLY MEMORY VERSES:
(II Corinthians)

- <u>Memorize One Verse Each Week As A Family</u> -

Week #1

"Not that we are sufficient of ourselves to think anything as of ourselves; but our sufficiency is of God." *II Corinthians 3:5*

Week #2

"Therefore if any man be in Christ, he is a new creature: old things are passed away; behold, all things are become new." *II Corinthians 5:17*

Week #3

"Be ye not unequally yoked together with unbelievers: for what fellowship hath righteousness with unrighteousness? and what communion hath light with darkness?" *II Corinthians 6:14*

Week #4

"But this I say, He which soweth sparingly shall reap also sparingly; and he which soweth bountifully shall reap also bountifully." *II Corinthians 9:6*

RESOURCES

1. The Bible Knowledge Commentary by Wolvoord and Zuck. (Victor Books, Wheaton, IL: 1986).

2. Liberty Bible Commentary Volume I by Hindson and Kroll(The Old-Time Gospel Hour, Lynchburg, VA: 1982).

3. Vines Expository Dictionary of New Testament Words by W.E. Vine, M.A. (Fleming H. Revell Co., Tappen, NJ: 1940).

4. Be Encouraged by Warren W. Wiersbe. (Victor Books, Wheaton, IL: 1984).

5. Second Epistle to the Corinthians by Charles J. Woodbridge. (The News, Curwensville, PA: 1958).

6. The Letters to the Corinthians (Revised Edition) by William Barclay. (Westminister John Knox Press, Louisville, KY: 1975).

7. The Life Application Bible (Tyndale House Publishers, Inc., Wheaton, IL: 1993).

ABOUT THE AUTHOR

⸺⸻

L ou Nicholes grew up on a small farm in southeastern
Ohio where his parents taught him the practical things
in life. In July 1954 while on a troop ship headed for
Germany, a navy chaplain led him to trust Jesus Christ as
his personal Saviour. Twenty-six hundred men were on
board the ship, and ten came to the meeting, but Lou was the
only one who responded to receive Christ.

It was at Philadelphia College of Bible, that Lou and I
met. We were married at my parents camp chapel in southern Illinois. At the end of Lou's senior year in college Paul
Bubar, from Word of Life Fellowship, came to speak at a
chapel service. He told us he had been asked by Jack
Wyrtzen to start a Bible club ministry for local churches. He
was recruiting missionaries to go to different parts of the
country. Lou knew this was his answer to prayer. He applied
and was accepted to pioneer the new Bible club program in
the mid-western United States.

It was a great experience for Lou to have a part in developing materials and programs for Bible clubs in local
churches. This included Bible studies, quiet-time diaries,
Scripture memory packs, followup materials, leadership
training programs etc. In addition to pioneering several

types of evangelistic outreaches, and starting a camp and Bible school scholarship program for those who wanted to excel in their spiritual growth, he also helped start a program called Teens Involved, which helps young people discover and develop their talents and abilities for the Lord.

God miraculously blessed with 262 Bible clubs in local churches, and approximately 1,200 laymen leading them. After twenty-six years, Lou turned this ministry over to other missionaries. He left the Midwest to pioneer a short-term missions program for Word of Life called Youth Reachout. For twelve years Lou trained and took over two thousand young people to forty-two countries around the world. The Lord worked through the lives of these young people as they ministered in churches, public schools, prisons, hospitals, orphanages, army bases, and many other types of evangelistic outreaches, including open-air evangelism. It was exciting and a privilege to see over forty thousand people of all ages make public decisions for Jesus Christ.

For the past few years, Lou and I have been given another door of opportunity, to pioneer. We are representatives for Word of Life in Asia and the South Pacific, where over sixty percent of the world's population is located in Asia alone. A high percentage of these are young people. We have had the opportunity to make various trips into this part of the world. The Lord is giving us unusual open doors to minister, make contacts, recruit potential staff, and help folks come for training so they can then go back to their countries to reach their people with the Gospel of Christ. We believe God is doing great and mighty things, and we are on the verge of one of the greatest adventures of our lives for His glory. God is so good!!!

With a grateful heart,
Thelma (Lou's Wife)

SAMPLE DAILY
COMMENTARY OUTLINE

Scripture Memory Verse for the week: _____

Today's Passage: _____

One Word Topic for the day: _____

What is the outstanding thought?

How do I make personal application in my life?

For More Information

If you would like to receive more information about other books and ministry resources produced by Lou Nicholes you can reach him by e-mail at lounicholes1@att.net or order books on the internet at www.XulonPress.com or www.Amazon.com

Other Books by the Author

The Bible in a Nutshell - 2003
Mark - *The Master Servant* - 2003
Numbers - *Wilderness Wanderings* - 2004
Acts - *The History of Missions* - 2004
Romans - *A Roadmap for the Christian Life* - 2004